Foreword by *New York Times* Bestselling Author

CHRIS BRADY

DEALING WITH DIFFICULT PEOPLE

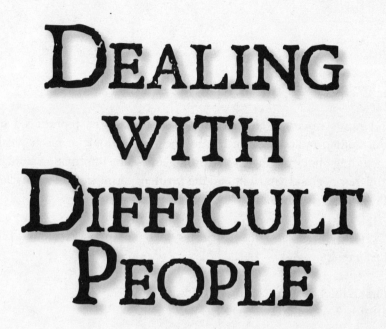

LIFE Leadership Essentials Series

OBSTACLÉS
PRESS

First Edition, August 2014
10 9 8 7 6 5 4 3 2 1

Published by:

Obstaclés Press
4072 Market Place Dr.
Flint, MI 48507

lifeleadership.com

ISBN 978-0-9904243-4-5

Cover design and layout by Norm Williams, nwa-inc.com

Printed in the United States of America

A man of character finds a special attractiveness in difficulty, since it is only by coming to grips with difficulty that he can realize his potentialities.

— CHARLES DE GAULLE

CONTENTS

FOREWORD

by Chris Brady

You feel the heat rising in your chest, and your fists clench. You are supposed to smile in this situation, but you just can't. Your blood pressure, if the pounding in your ears is any indication, is likely high. You can't believe it, but you're back in this position again with that particular person who just seems to know how to push your buttons and make you want to fight.

Or you want to run and hide. The fight-or-flight instinct within you chooses the latter, and you can't wait to leave the room. In fact, you'd fall right through the floor if you could, just to get away from *that person*.

What is it about certain people? Why are we unable to behave appropriately around them? Why are they so argumentative? Why are they so mean? Rude? Disrespectful? Selfish? And even more important, what are *you* supposed to do about it?

We've all been in situations like this—likely too numerous to count. For whatever reason, no matter how we try, there will just be times in life when we are challenged by having to interact with people who are difficult at best and downright hateful at worst. Sometimes they are in our workplace, sometimes in our neighborhood, and even sometimes in our family. Make no mistake about it: difficult people will find their way into your life time and time again.

In surveying the field of literature on the subject of human relations, one is confronted by the immense amount of material targeted toward marriages, dating, and family. There are many more on developing people skills and how to communicate. Common also are books on temperaments, personalities, tendencies, and various other classifications all designed to make it easier to understand, and therefore get along with, others. But largely missing from the marketplace is material dealing directly with this touchy issue of difficult people in general and conflict in particular. There just doesn't seem to be much available on the subject. Perhaps this is because it's not a "fun" topic, or maybe it's because there are no easy answers to how to handle one's self in the presence of perpetually hard-to-get-along-with people. Neither of these reasons negates the need, however, for a clear, accurate, and practical guide on how to navigate such treacherous waters. And that is where this book fits. While certainly not exhaustive on the subject, nor the final say, this book does pack in a lot of useful, practical advice about how to spot difficult people, understand a little bit more about why they behave the way they do, and most productive of all, respond accordingly. Interestingly, it also begins with how to avoid becoming a difficult person oneself!

So turn the page, get ready to pull back the curtain on those challenging times in human interaction, and begin equipping yourself with the tools to not only emerge unscathed but actually better for the experience. Believe it or not, in many instances, if properly handled, difficult people can be turned into productive partners. It's not easy. But it is worth it. And this book shows you how.

Chris Brady
CEO and Creative Director of LIFE Leadership

INTRODUCTION

You cannot swim for new horizons until
you have the courage to lose sight of the shore.
— WILLIAM FAULKNER

Some things in life are certain. It is proverbial that everyone has to deal with death and taxes, and a whole law — Murphy's Law, to be exact — is dedicated to explaining the various mishaps that come in the course of everyday living. In addition to these and other laws of existence, one thing is absolutely sure:

You are going to encounter difficult people during your life.

This is true. It's going to happen. But instead of just waiting around for it to come and then responding in shock like a deer in headlights or getting emotional and lashing out, good leaders learn to take action now — before difficulties arise. They know they'll have to deal with some difficult people, so they tackle it head on. In fact, a great plaque reads:

Live
Love
Laugh

This is fantastic advice, but it's not the plaque we want to address. The other plaque, one we all need to study and internalize, reads:

> *You are going to encounter difficult people.*
> *Plan on it.*
> *Prepare for it.*
> *Become good at it.*

That's what this book is going to teach you: how to be good at dealing with difficult people. But before we start, let's get personal for a minute.

> **You are going to encounter difficult people. Plan on it.**

Think of the most difficult person you've ever had to deal with. Picture this person in your mind. What did he or she say or do that was so difficult to take? Why do you still remember this event now? Why did it leave such an impression? What did you say to the person? What *should* you have said or done?

Now think of another difficult person. Again, why is this person so memorable? And how do you wish you had handled your interaction differently?

While we don't mean to start you mentally replaying all the memorable encounters you've had with difficult people and looping all the words you could have said to them in your mind—over and over—we recognize that everyone has had a few such experiences. And frankly, we're all probably in for a few more as we go about our business in life.

For example, have you met the Diva? She is so sure she's the best thing that ever happened to you that she wants to be treated with all sorts of perks, benefits, and special rewards—even before she's started working with you.

Or the Boss, who criticizes everything you do and the way you do it because he's convinced that he always has a better answer? Or have you met the Bureaucrat, who uses rules and regulations against you like a cannon? Common sense is irrelevant to such a person, who seems to delight in making your life more difficult.

Or have you had to deal with the Victim, the Autocrat, or the Bungee Jumper? All these types of difficult people can make life very frustrating unless you recognize what they are doing and know how to turn your interaction to something positive—even wonderful.

The truth is that really effective leaders know how to deal with difficult people—even with the Politician, who smiles and flatters you to your face and then organizes a network of gossip, undermining behaviors, and ongoing drama behind your back. This type of difficult person is enough to frustrate pretty much anyone, unless you know how to effectively take the right kind of action.

Whatever kind of difficult people you face in life, this book will teach you the principles of turning difficulties into success. Because whether the difficult people you encounter are good people who simply have strong personalities, those who genuinely need help or institutionalization, or anything in between, we all have to deal with difficult people at some point.

And for most of us, this will be a recurring event, not just a once-in-a-lifetime, laugh-it-off occurrence.

Learning how to smoothly and effectively deal with such personalities and situations is a leadership skill that we all need under our belts. In fact, once you can turn potentially difficult relationships with people into well-functioning, successful ones, you'll find yourself achieving a lot more in life, with a lot less stress, hassle, and overall difficulty.

You'll also find that people you might previously have written off as too bossy, opinionated, moody, rude, talkative, or any other kind of "difficult" can actually be some of your top performers and greatest allies. And even if they stay difficult, you can learn how to best respond and most effectively get on with the really important matters in your life.

Frankly, some people who are "difficult" are totally worth putting up with! And when we need to interact with those who accomplish much less along with their difficulty, we're still further ahead when we can make things *less* difficult with them.

In short, you're going to encounter difficult people. Some of them will be among your best friends and most beneficial partners, while others have the potential to make your life harder.

In either case, it's incredibly helpful to learn how to effectively deal with them—and not just because it will make your life easier. It will also make you a better leader and, frankly, a better person.

But this will only happen if you know what to do and how to do it well. If you, like most people, haven't given much thought to dealing with difficult people, you'll most likely be a sitting duck when one comes along.

Many of the most committed difficult people — the ones who actually *like* being difficult and do it on purpose — count on you and others to remain easy targets.

Effective leaders understand this, and they know what to do about it. When they are confronted by a difficult person or situation, they quickly assess what is happening, determine what type of difficult person they are dealing with, and launch into the Five-Step Peace Process — turning difficulty into progress.

In the chapters ahead, you'll learn what such leaders know: how to effectively deal with difficult people. You'll also learn how to avoid being a difficult person yourself, since almost all of us have moments when we are more difficult than we should be.

You're going to learn how to deal with difficult people following the same pattern top leaders use. First, in part one of this book, you'll learn seven main types of difficult people — because understanding why they're being difficult is essential to knowing how to properly and effectively respond. Then, in part two, you'll learn the Five-Step Peace Process of dealing successfully with each difficult person who crosses your path.

Most important, you'll learn how to make sure that difficult people don't have the power and that *you* do. As Roman emperor Marcus Aurelius, who dealt with more than his share of difficult people, put it: "It is not the actions of others that trouble us."[1] It's how we deal with difficulties that determines our success.

The way you respond to difficult people makes all the difference, and while most people unwittingly give away most of their own personal power when faced with difficult people, top leaders maintain their power and use it to help those around them. Again, they identify what type of difficult person they are dealing with, and then they use the principles of the Five-Step Peace Process to respond appropriately.

So keep reading. Anyone who wishes to become a top leader needs to learn and master this wisdom and these skills. Who knows? The next difficult person in your life might be right around the corner. Or maybe he or she won't show up for a long time. Either way, knowing how to effectively deal with difficult people will make you a better person, friend, family member, and leader.

PART ONE

Seven Types of Difficult People

There are at least seven major types of difficult people, and knowing which you are dealing with at any given time is essential information for leaders. Without it, your response to a difficult person is usually hit or miss. Each of the seven types is unique and interesting. They are all difficult for their own reasons and in their own ways.

As you learn about these and other kinds of difficult people, keep in mind that the Five-Step Peace Process will help you deal with each one — though in different ways.

Now, let's start with a really important technique: Smile as you read and learn about the seven types of difficult people. You may find some old friends in these chapters. You may even find that you resemble some of these characters. If so, apply what top leader Chris Brady calls the first great rule of dealing with difficult people: Don't be a difficult person yourself!

For best results, don't read about these seven types of difficult people in a spirit of judgment, but rather with humor and respect. People who are difficult might not even realize that they are, or they may be struggling to change. This book will be a lot more fun if you laugh as you learn about each kind. They're all pretty funny, truth be told. (And don't forget: Even though we may refer to the Diva as "she" or the Boss as "he," each one of the types comes in all varieties of people. There are plenty of male Divas and female Bosses.)

Smile. Laugh. Learn.

Knowledge of the seven main types of difficult people will be very helpful in life, but don't take yourself too seriously as you learn about them. If you find yourself shouting at the imaginary people in the chapter about the Diva, the Politician, or any of the others, you need to relax. Be less difficult. Have more fun.

This book is meant to be enjoyable!

Start by taking a big, deep breath. Now smile widely.

Okay, let's begin.

CHAPTER 1

The Diva

She might have seen that what bowed her head so profoundly—
the thought of the world's concern at her situation—was
founded on illusion. She was not an existence, an experience,
a passion, a structure of sensations, to anybody but herself.
To all humankind besides, Tess was only a passing thought.
—THOMAS HARDY

Jacob was at his wits' end. How could anyone really be
like this?

He had been conducting interviews for someone to fill his old
spot, since he'd been asked to head up the company's brand-new
research and development department. He was responsible for
promoting someone in-house to fill the vacancy caused by his
own promotion.

He'd been working for this opportunity for as long as he could
remember, and now he just needed to make this one hire so he
could get to work on his new responsibilities. Everything had
been going great until Sacia's meeting came up.

Jacob was actually the one who had interviewed her originally for her current job. Remembering this gave him a little bit of clarity.

At first, her résumé seemed promising, but the longer her interview went, the more puzzled Jacob felt. And by the end, he was left totally annoyed, a bit disgusted, and utterly confused about what to do next.

Yes, she had an impressive résumé, but instead of living up to it, she kept pointing at it and asking him invasive questions about his own credentials. Interestingly, another interviewee, Mike, had similarly emphasized his past work, but somehow he seemed to have an aura of leadership and initiative in the way he handled the interview.

Sacia, however, seemed to expect him to give her the job, or maybe even his own job or his boss's job, just because she had good test scores in elementary school and assured him she had lots of potential.

Rather than coming across as bold, tenacious, or resourceful, she seemed to be sneering at him for not knowing who she was, and then she turned the interview on him to see if he was in the "in." Who did he know? She dropped names from her long list of contacts.

Finally, to top it off, she haughtily explained how other companies would probably be courting her soon and that she could only possibly work for this firm if the owner himself came and personally asked her to join the team — naturally offering a great office and a paycheck double what Jacob made!

Jacob was left dazed and confused by the experience because on the surface, she had displayed the qualities he liked to see in an interview — confidence, poise, initiative, the works! — except she came across as smug and arrogant.

Other than being demanding, superior, and impressed with herself, she actually didn't seem to have much to offer the company. But what if he was wrong? If this was her way of showing bold and innovative action, did he want to miss out on the opportunity to bring her into the company?

After reflection, he decided to take a risk on her. He managed to get her the meeting with the CEO — he was still rather proud of his resourcefulness at making that happen — and she came on board.

Unfortunately, he'd seen nothing since that time to make him feel it had been worth it, and there had been much to make him regret the political capital he'd spent getting her in.

Yet this second interview had been almost a perfect repeat of the first one! "Why is she so difficult?" he found himself asking the empty office aloud.

Introducing the Diva

Have you ever met someone who was so convinced of her own specialness that she went around demanding tribute from all who gazed upon her? If so, in all likelihood, you were dealing with the Diva.

The Diva is the person who has to talk to your supervisor, not because there's anything wrong with you, but because she thinks she deserves to be speaking with someone with a bigger office and a fancier car — someone on what she perceives to be closer to her *own* level.

She's the minor celebrity who expects to be treated like the world's biggest star when she scores her first appearance as a backup dancer in a music video or an extra in a second-rate film. This is the girl who sends her hamburger back three times so she can get the tomatoes cut just right or have the proper number of sesame seeds put on the bun.

All in all, the Diva, what some people would call a "poser," is characterized by being needy, picky, and a little too impressed with her own merit—often without real results. She is generally someone who's done *something* and thinks it was way more important than it actually was.

She also happens to expect everyone to be showering her with flowery compliments, special treatment, and exaggerated credit for what she's done—or worse, just for who she is or even for who she knows.

One Good Deed = A Lifetime of Bragging Rights

Like Tinker Bell from Disney's *Peter Pan*,[1] the ugly stepsisters from the story of Cinderella,[2] or the Queen of Hearts from Lewis Carroll's *Alice's Adventures in Wonderland*,[3] the Diva has an overly inflated sense of accomplishment or personal merit and demands a certain level of respect and recognition for it, without being concerned about earning a positive reputation, working hard for distinction, or even treating others with respect.

The Diva thinks everyone should recognize her name and treat her in ways she supposedly earned back in the day, but she often doesn't walk the walk anymore, if she ever did.

The Diva feels that because of who she is, where she comes from, or what she once did (or plans to do soon), she ought to be revered, respected, and reverenced on a level above those around her. She wants special treatment.

While some Divas have actually accomplished important results, they are notorious for expecting others to realize how special they are without them having to continue performing at high levels and for equating their own accomplishments with the much *greater* accomplishments of genuine top leaders and highly successful people.

The Pecking Order Rules

The Diva recognizes the head honcho and thinks herself his equal. She demands to be recognized by him as such and treasured by "the inferiors" with the same degree of respect.

She tends to see the world as a pecking order. Accordingly, she expects everyone to bend over backward to get her whatever she wants, no matter how bizarre or difficult to come by and no matter how little she's done to earn such treatment.

Good Diva / Bad Diva

There is a certain type of Diva who, unlike most, actually continues to *perform* at high and valuable levels rather than expecting one good deed to pretty much cover her for the rest of her life.

This kind of Diva is still difficult because she continues to demand special treatment and expect a certain level of reverence and recognition from those around her. But the fact that she makes a point of *earning* special treatment makes her a whole different breed from those who want it for nothing.

While she may still be picky, needy, and very open about the fact that she expects to get what she wants when she wants it, this type of Diva can be a valuable asset because she actually walks the walk. She doesn't just expect to receive glory; she intends to work very hard for it and continually does so.

When you get a Diva who's willing to put her money — and, more important, her actions — where her mouth is, she's often worth the hassle of making her feel appreciated and taken care of. The lesson from this type of Diva is simple: Don't be this way, no matter how valuable you are.

Diva World

Most types of Divas, the ones who just want everyone to jump through hoops for them without bringing anything worthwhile to the table, are usually difficult and less than helpful. But there are ways to deal with them that will make it much easier to turn any situation more positive.

Learning to deal with Divas in general will save a whole lot of time and energy that might otherwise be spent running to different grocery stores trying to find the right brand of bottled water for someone who still hasn't learned to tie her own shoes.

But first, before we discuss how to deal with Diva difficulty, let's learn about other main types of difficult people.

Mirror Workshop

Look in the mirror and look yourself right in the eyes. Ask yourself sincerely: "Am I a Diva at work? At home? At my kid's soccer games? Anywhere?"

Answer honestly.

If your answer is yes to any of the above, stop. Change. Don't be a Diva any longer.

We'll learn later in this book how to deal with difficult people, but the first rule is vital: Don't be a Diva yourself.

CHAPTER 2

The Boss

*Blessed is the man who, having nothing to say, abstains
from giving us wordy evidence of the fact.*
—GEORGE ELIOT

Karen sat with her arms folded as Jeremy explained for the
fifth time the importance of her purchasing life insurance — this
week, if possible! Imagine if something were to happen; how
would she be leaving her family?

As the source of a huge portion of their income, she — along
with Rob — was their biggest asset, and if something were to
happen to her, heaven forbid, she would be leaving those kids
in a terrible situation of not only grief but also complete financial ruin!

It might make sense if he were an insurance salesman with an
appointment to get her to buy something from him or if she had
asked his advice about the topic — or anything! But no, this was
just Jeremy.

He'd been working in the cubicle next to her for just over a
month now, and telling her how to live her life seemed to be his
favorite pastime. Last week, it had been the evils of gluten, and

the week before, it was the absolute necessity of transferring her kids to a different school (there was actually something to this one; she'd have to talk to Rob about it sometime).

"Honestly, Karen, I think you're being irresponsible about this. As a mother, you absolutely owe it to your kids to look out for their interests. You're just being selfish and silly to not consider the possibilities and plan for the worst-case scenario. I'm genuinely surprised at you!"

Jeremy interrupted her thoughts by stopping his lecture. She nodded and gave a noncommittal response; hopefully he'd get distracted by something else before he got to the point of eliciting a commitment from her to talk to some specialist or whatever he had lined up to fix her gross neglect this time. No such luck.

"Well?" he asked pointedly.

"Well, what?" Karen returned.

"Well, are you ready to actually do something about this now, or are you determined to ruin their futures? Remember, this isn't about you; it's about those kids of yours! Karen, you need to stop putting this off. It's just not fair to them. Stop being so selfish and get this done!

"I know a guy who can give you some numbers, and he said he'd be happy to meet with you this weekend. I told him you get off at 6:30 (just to be safe), and he's expecting your call. Here's his card. Will you promise to call him?"

Karen sighed. She wished she could get some work done. Jeremy's constant diatribes about her life made it difficult to concentrate. She dreaded coming to work at all.

Introducing the Boss

We've all met this guy. He's the backseat driver who won't shut up and even grabs the wheel sometimes to ensure that you make the right turn. He's the brother-in-law who can't stop telling you how to raise your kids or treat your spouse. He's the neighbor who has to make sure you contribute the right things to the community in the right ways and on his time schedule.

He's characterized by his dictatorial, in-your-face, and in-your-business attitude toward life, and he seems to have no fear of stepping on toes or putting his nose where it doesn't belong. He's not really helping you, though many of his ideas might actually be beneficial if he shared them effectively.

The Boss has confidence in his own opinions and abilities to the point of arrogance and very little trust in anybody else's. He is full of disdain for you and everyone else — except himself.

Because of this, he seems to think it's his duty, or at least his right, to tell everyone else what they've missed in their own assessment of any and all situations. He often comes off as outspoken, insensitive, and extremely pushy. He seems to have no sense of personal boundaries because he thinks his superior understanding of every situation puts him above you and others.

Loud Unsolicited Advice

Like Lady Catherine de Bourgh from Jane Austen's *Pride and Prejudice*,[1] Rachel Lynde from L. M. Montgomery's

Anne of Green Gables,[2] or Ted from the 1996 movie *Jingle All the Way*,[3] the Boss thinks it's his job, his life mission, and his business to tell you what yours is and should be. In essence, this guy is what the world would call bossy.

He has no qualms about telling people what to do and how to do it, and he isn't afraid to step in and tell you all the ways you're wrong in life—even if he has no actual authority over you and no real understanding of your situation, family, or work, even if you never ask, and even if you tell him to stop.

While the Boss is sometimes right and even helpful with his advice, he is notorious for offering it at unsolicited and unwanted moments, without concern or consideration for natural boundaries or other people's rights or feelings.

When you're dealing with the Boss, you probably have moments of clarity where you realize he's making some good points, but you can't help wondering what on earth this guy is doing in your space harassing you about your own business and personal life.

The longer you know the Boss, the more difficult you find it to listen or care about his "counsel" because he tends to leave you feeling that he is totally out of line to have initiated the conversation at all, no matter how firm his grasp of the situation.

Insight Makes Right?

The Boss often compares people's failures to what he thinks they *should* have been—according to his own way of doing things.

Anytime people are struggling to do a hard or stressful task, you can be sure the Boss will be along to tell them how they should do it, how *he* would do it (or how he *would* have done it), and how much better the outcome would be — rather than offering meaningful sympathy or authentic help.

The Boss often says things like "It's not that I'm tyrannical or controlling." Then he implies, "It's just that I'm so much better at everything than anyone I've ever met." Yet he's often more concerned with telling others how to behave or act than with using his capabilities to accomplish real and meaningful achievements himself. In fact, he usually doesn't accomplish much at all himself. He's too focused on counseling others.

But the Boss isn't necessarily trying to be mean or rude. He just can't keep his opinions, observations, or advice to himself.

"Thanks, Boss!"

In some cases, people who learn to correctly handle the Boss will find him to be a great ally, if he actually has a knack for seeing what's wrong with the situation and how to make it better.

One rare version of the Boss is extremely competent and intuitively brilliant. This type is worth learning to deal with because he can often provide powerful and insightful advice on how to better achieve goals or accomplish important objectives.

While he brings his fair share of trouble and drama, this effective version of the Boss also pulls his weight in getting tasks done. Likewise, his ability to see what's wrong and how to fix it and his willingness to speak his mind on important challenges can be turned into real assets.

This helpful type of Boss can be a powerful part of the team if leaders learn to incorporate his strengths and effectively counter his weaknesses. When the Boss finds his niche and synergizes with the team, his difficulty is worth the frustration because he also brings needed insight to the table.

But in contrast, like the lower-end Divas, the other versions of the Boss are more difficult because they're less helpful. Learning to effectively deal with them will save a lot of time, energy, and hassle.

Mirror Workshop

The first thing to do if you have a Boss in your life is to ask yourself if anything he or she is telling you is actually helpful. If so, write it down, think about it, and make a plan of action to improve.

Truth and good ideas can be very beneficial, even when they come from a surprising source.

CHAPTER 3

The Bureaucrat

*Any fool can make a rule, and any
fool will mind it.*
—HENRY DAVID THOREAU

Emily wiped her tears and resolutely walked out of the bathroom. Normally, she wouldn't cry over something so silly. She would just handle it in the moment and be done, but with the baby on the way, her emotions had been on the fritz. "Ridiculous!" she told herself.

In fact, the whole thing was ridiculous, not just the fact that she was crying – again!

She had been sitting there beside Ada at the after-school program she volunteered for through her church. Ada was her eight-year-old next-door neighbor whose mother had been struggling since her husband left a few weeks before.

Emily had agreed to take Ada along with her to the activity, but with all the stress and confusion going on in her life, little Ada was afraid to go sit with the kids her own age.

Since she was only a year older than the group Emily was working with and didn't know anyone else, Emily decided to bring her along with the seven-year-olds. That way, she'd have a positive experience, and once she felt more comfortable, she'd be excited to meet the other girls in her own group.

That's when Melanie, the supervisor of the girl groups, came up and took matters into her own hands. She had met Ada a time or two with her mother. But she really didn't have a relationship with her and wasn't aware of what the girl had been through over the last few weeks.

Thinking back, Emily couldn't believe the way Melanie had just grabbed Ada by the arm and dragged her out of the room to take her to the older group. Emily tried to stop her, explaining that it was okay. Ada could stay with her today; they'd worked the whole thing out. But Melanie quickly informed her that Ada needed to be where she was supposed to be.

"She's eight, so she has to be with the eight-year-olds. She can't be with the seven-year-olds."

That was when little Ada started to cry.

Still tugging the crying child by the arm and trying to get away from Emily's concerned words, Melanie walked out of the room and marched down the hall.

Then the pregnancy tears started for Emily, and she headed for the bathroom, leaving the other girls with another volunteer. She wiped her tears for just a moment before she realized this was bigger than her. She had to make this right for Ada. Otherwise, the little girl might never come back, and the interaction with these other girls was something she desperately needed in her life right now.

Emily quickly left the bathroom. When she caught up to Melanie and Ada, they were in another bathroom themselves, so Ada could wipe her tears. Melanie was trying to explain to the girl that she couldn't always stay with her mom and needed to stop relying on family so much and get out into the world – that it was "part of growing up."

"Great," thought Emily. "That's exactly what she doesn't need right now: less faith in the stability of her family." So she asked Ada to wait in the hall for a moment and, still crying a bit, broached the topic with Melanie.

The more they talked, the more Emily was flabbergasted at how strictly Melanie tried to stick to the rules, even though there was clearly something higher at stake here.

No matter how Emily answered each objection, Melanie repeated again and again that what mattered most was for the girl to be where she was "supposed to be." Melanie held firm: "She's eight, not seven."

Finally, Emily asked, "Let me see if I've got this right. You think it's more important for her to be with other eight-year-olds than to find value in coming to these meetings, even though she's likely to associate all church functions with the experience she has here today?"

Melanie didn't miss a beat. "She'll never be happy at church unless she's forced to go where she belongs."

Catching herself from responding too quickly, Emily looked at the other woman for a moment. "What now?" she asked herself. She knew this was a pivotal moment for Ada, but Melanie wouldn't budge. "What now?"

Rulers' Rules Rule!

The Bureaucrat is the type of difficult person who fights tooth and nail for the rules and regulations, protecting and worshiping the world's red tape above anything else. If you've encountered this type of difficult person, you'll never forget it.

The Bureaucrat is the librarian who won't let you return books at the desk if there's an outdoor book drop. She's the neighbor who comes to tell you it's not okay to have that many wind chimes in your backyard—not because they keep her or anyone awake but just because "everyone knows that one or two wind chimes are enough." She's the bus driver who won't let your kids sit together on the way to school because they're different ages.

In short, the Bureaucrat is the person who's given her allegiance to policy, rules, convention, tradition, or what's "supposed to be," even when it arbitrarily throws reason, sense, caring, and actual benefit to the wind.

The Bureaucrat is characterized by being rules-oriented even when the rules don't apply anymore, unconcerned with the spirit of the law, and totally unconscious of *why* things matter (or at least unwilling to put the needs of the individual first). Unfortunately, like the Boss, she often has a tendency to try to enforce her opinion of what "ought to be" on other people, and she often forgets to consider differences in situations, needs, or unique individuals.

For the Bureaucrat, it's not about what's really good or best in a given situation—because the rules are *always* good and best.

Like Javert from Victor Hugo's *Les Misérables*,[1] Tuvok from *Star Trek: Voyager*,[2] or Sebastian from Disney's *The Little Mermaid*,[3] to the Bureaucrat, rules are everything. The rules might even be bad (for example, China's mandatory abortion policies or Hitler's anti-Semitic laws). But to the Bureaucrat, rules are rules, and they're not to be questioned by regular people.

Sometimes the Bureaucrat deliberately hides behind the rules for personal gain or to avoid following her conscience, but more often, she genuinely thinks following the rules no matter what will make everyone happier and better off in the long run.

"Correct" = Right?

For the Bureaucrat, the rules (including customs, traditions, social norms, etc.) are never wrong; they always apply to everyone, no matter the circumstances. And it's always her duty to inform other people of the rules and attempt to force them to behave "properly."

While she doesn't always (but sometimes *does*) realize it, some of her governing ideas and core values are: "This is where you're supposed to be"; "Stay where you belong"; "If there's a line, get in it—regardless of where it goes—at the back!"; and "Do what you're told."

To the Bureaucrat, if you're following orders, obeying the rules, and staying where you belong, no questions asked, you are doing the right thing. For her, life is about doing your job, helping others do theirs by reminding them of their place, and otherwise not stepping on any toes.

No Flexibility

The Bureaucrat seeks to find her place in society and stick to it without allowing anyone else to mess with boundaries or roles and also without questioning or challenging authority herself. If she considers you beneath her in the pecking order or in some way under her jurisdiction, she's almost certain to come at you and try to control your life with whatever rules she thinks you aren't living to the letter, even if there's a good reason you're breaking those supposed rules.

Levels of Bureaucracy

Very often, a person who gets caught up in this mentality goes too far, and rigid thinking takes over. The idea is to get rid of human error, even though you are dealing with people. Obviously, this sometimes causes extra difficulty. But there are still differences in the various Bureaucratic types, and some are better than others.

For example, someone who is genuinely trying to be good and helpful but simply has a skewed worldview is obviously a better, less malicious person—if not particularly less difficult to deal with—than one who intentionally uses the rules and policies to twist people's arms and get them to "stand in line" in order for the Bureaucrat to achieve personal successes or benefit due to the subservience of others. The Bureaucrat who just loves power may be the worst of all.

Whenever you deal with any kind of Bureaucrat, you may be in for a tough time. This type of difficult person can be especially frustrating for some people because logic, reason, and common sense seem to have no place in the conversation. That's the crux of dealing with the Bureaucrat.

Mirror Workshop

In part two, we're going to learn how to deal with difficult people of all types. Here's a little peek ahead: One of the early steps in dealing with a difficult person is identifying which type he or she most closely resembles. This gives you a powerful head start in turning difficulty into something much better. For now, pay close attention to each of the seven main types because this will help you deal more effectively with difficult people — as we'll learn later. Quiz yourself: What are the main characteristics of the Diva? The Boss? The Bureaucrat?

CHAPTER 4

The Victim

*I can choose either to be a victim of the world or
an adventurer in search of treasure. It's all a
question of how I view my life.*
—PAULO COELHO

Jared resisted the urge to slap his palm to his forehead in amazement. Seriously? Did Lance realize what he'd just said? Jared looked around the room and saw that Mary and Cathy were equally incredulous. None of the others seemed to notice. They probably just didn't know Lance well enough to put two and two together.

It had been several months since Lance came on board, but he still hadn't brought much to the table, despite big promises and countless quotes on how it was important to judge a man by his results, not his words.

But the fact that Lance was continually saying how much he was going to do, ironically summing it all up at the end with a great speech on how "actions speak louder than words" or "a picture is worth a thousand words," but never doing it wasn't the worst part. No, that wasn't the worst at all!

The worst part was that after everything they'd been through, all their hard work, Lance had the nerve to walk into this meeting and tell their supervisor that nobody was really working — that the reason they hadn't met their quota this month was because they simply didn't have the leadership in their region to make things really fly!

After everything that Jared and Cathy had both given and offered this quarter, it was almost beyond offensive. Or at least it would have been, if they didn't know Lance. As it was, it was more ridiculous, even if still a little shocking, to hear such inconsistency and almost brutal hypocrisy.

That's where Jared stopped himself. Sitting around getting really mad about Lance wouldn't help anything, and Lance wasn't actually some evil person. He was just a guy — generally a good-natured, enthusiastic guy who just couldn't seem to figure out that he was the one getting in his own way.

At this point in his mental reframe, Jared's attention turned back to what the group was discussing. Nathan, their director, was making some great points about how important it was to just keep working toward the goals, even though they hadn't met theirs this time.

Jared glanced over to see Lance fervently nodding, and he hoped he wouldn't feel the need to say anything else. No such luck.

Lance raised his hand, and when Nathan called on him, Lance started explaining how he was trying very hard to meet the goal, but he just couldn't get anyone in his pod to work with him! To hear him tell it, Lance was the hardest worker around, and everyone else was wimpy, afraid, and lazy.

Jared wasn't worried about what Nathan would think; he was a smart enough leader to recognize what kind of person he was dealing with. But this wasn't the only time Lance's attitude had come up. Last week, he had done the same thing in front of a whole group of trainees – trainees Jared was responsible for.

It was one thing to deal with Lance's accusations and complaints when they were with Nathan, but when they were with the new people, it was something else entirely. That kind of thinking could seriously damage the whole environment of their business, especially if Lance could manage to make a culture of it.

Unfortunately, when it came down to it, it was Jared's job to make sure that didn't happen. But what was he supposed to do with Lance?

Remember Him?

You know that guy with the "poor me" attitude who mopes around complaining about how the whole world did him wrong, blames others for his problems, and thinks everyone with success just got lucky? Yep, that's the Victim.

He's the guy who sits around all day and then complains about how his wife never has the house clean or his meals ready on time. He's the guy who listens to his leader's explanation of some of the difficulties happening in the team and, rather than looking at how he can change himself, sits nodding and pointing at all the people in the room who he thinks need to shape up.

He's the guy who gets enthusiastic when he finds a way to blame others but is frustrated and negative the rest of the time. And of course, he's the guy who can't move on when people hurt his feelings or don't treat him the way he wanted them to. Instead, he complains about how his opportunities are taken away by others and excuses himself from taking any responsibility for himself or doing anything at all.

The Victim is often characterized by a lack of introspective capability and an inability or unwillingness to recognize his own power or responsibility to influence the outcome of his life. He tends to believe that he's never done anything wrong and that everyone or anyone else is to blame for his failings or unfortunate circumstances. If he isn't where he wants to be in life, it's because the world, or someone in it, stole his chance of getting there or he just hasn't gotten lucky yet. When someone else succeeds, he says something like "Wow! I wish I were that lucky. Some people get all the luck." And he seems to really believe this.

Like Eeyore from A. A. Milne's *Winnie the Pooh*,[1] the Victim doesn't seem to see that other people are living their lives for themselves — not specifically to bother or hurt him — or that he has a chance to do the same!

The Victim is rarely able to see any possible association between his problems and his actions, so he almost never takes the actions necessary to produce better circumstances or results. Instead, he takes the faults of others personally and thinks his own are inconsequential or nonexistent.

Me, Me, Me

The Victim can often be heard saying things like "Why me?"; "Poor me"; "If only they would…"; and "I wish someone had…"; and he generally reacts to pretty much anything the world throws at him with thoughts of how someone else could make it better, if only he or she were willing.

He generally feels sorry for what he isn't achieving or getting, but he very rarely sees any connection between his circumstances and his own power to make things happen. It's all about everyone else.

The Victim believes anything anyone else does is all about him, and things that aren't happening but should be are someone else's fault. Not only does he worry that everyone else is probably out to get him, but he also believes that he's seldom if ever at fault for anything that goes wrong. In his mind, he has few weaknesses or faults, and everyone else's weaknesses and faults, as well as their strengths and successes, are targeted to hurt him or somehow block his luck.

Too often when the Victim hears a speech, reads a book, or comes in contact with someone who teaches how to overcome the very weaknesses he struggles with, he recognizes the problems and nods fervently about how true the words are about other people with those weaknesses, but he doesn't seem to recognize that the speech, book, or conversation would help him personally.

To the surprise of everyone around him, the Victim can often be heard complaining about "those people" and explaining at great length what they do that they shouldn't or don't do that they should—perfectly describing his own failings and shortcomings without realizing the irony of the situation. Interestingly, he often tends to lash out against others for the very same worst habits and behaviors that he displays, without ever seeming to make the connection.

The Victim is almost always guilty of gross inaction toward the goals, dreams, and pursuits he truly cares about, and yet this is exactly what he accuses others of and shakes his head at when he sees it. You might even hear him lecturing on the evils of those who "talk the talk but don't walk the walk," though this is precisely his own tendency.

In short, the Victim has a very clear understanding of the problem with not putting your money where your mouth is, but he doesn't realize that this is his own weakness. Instead, he points fingers and assigns blame to all those "underactive people" he believes are ruining his chance at success (usually those closest to him, even if they are working very hard).

Good Victim / Bad Victim

While the Victim mentality is never good, there are some individuals who could fall under the label of "the Victim" who are considerably less difficult and much more helpful than others in the same category.

The main difference between high-functioning Victims and the truly difficult ones is almost always the level at which they're able to genuinely listen to good mentors and apply their advice to themselves.

One of the main weaknesses and blind spots of pretty much every Victim is a lack of effective introspection, so they almost always need a wise, willing, and loving mentor to help them realize where they fall short and assist them with finding appropriate solutions. Victims who submit to great mentoring and push themselves to apply the teachings and counsel of their mentors will be less difficult and function at a higher level to the extent that they do so. Over time, this process can help them stop being Victims altogether.

Those Victim types who don't make such changes will likely continue to see others as the problem and will rarely make any progress in their ability to see their own weaknesses or engage their own power to overcome them.

Mirror Workshop

All of us, no matter who we are, can benefit from asking our mentor the following question: "What would you consider to be my biggest blind spot, the number-one thing I can and should change but may not realize is a concern?"

Have this conversation with your mentor. Be genuine, listen humbly, and don't be defensive or take offense. Once your mentor has shared this blind spot with you, ask him or her for recommendations on how to overcome it. Then follow your mentor's advice.

Work on this, and put in the effort and consistency to turn this weakness into a strength. Oh, and one other thing: Don't play the Victim if you don't like the response your mentor gives you!

CHAPTER 5

The Autocrat

*In a victory speech, I like to thank
the opposition, because without their
help, I couldn't have won.*
—JAROD KINTZ

Bill put down his laser pointer and looked around the room for questions. Teresa's hand shot up right away. "I have a big problem with this," she said, shaking her head worriedly.

Bill saw where this was headed and reminded himself mentally: "I should have mentioned something about this plan to her before I shared the proposal with the whole group. Too late now."

He patiently asked her about her concerns, but rather than addressing specific issues in the proposal, she kept talking about how the whole plan was flawed, how it would never work with their customers, and how they'd be wasting valuable time and manpower trying to implement it when it was inevitably going to fail.

Bill couldn't help but smile a little inside. Teresa was truly brilliant at this. She was very articulate and great at swaying *people. She suggested alternatives that she liked better and outlined her general concerns. And without going into any detail, she made it seem like his entire proposal was clearly flawed in every way. Masterful.*

She didn't really win friends with her talks; she was too abrasive for that. But she did bring a spirit of contention that left people feeling uneasy about any plan or proposal. Bill had tried to discuss each point with her during such outbursts in the past, but he had learned that this only escalated her negativity and would ruin any chance of getting the plan started.

Watching the way Teresa controlled the opinions of the people in the room was sometimes fun — she was genuinely gifted — yet it was starting to impact their productivity and overall progress. They hadn't gotten anywhere in weeks!

Besides, her gifts seemed limited to tearing down a plan or getting support for her own — seldom lending any strength to someone else's work. "My idea or bad idea" appeared to be her motto.

Bill had tried questioning her to find out what exactly she didn't like, but at this point, he was pretty sure she didn't even know herself. She was sure nothing they'd come up with had any chance of working, yet she couldn't say exactly why and wouldn't talk about what options would work. She much preferred to discuss — at length — the fact that the current plan was a bad idea, and Bill was starting to worry she was doing it just for fun.

Not that she appeared to be having fun. Not at all. But she did this consistently enough that Bill wondered if she actually enjoyed the process. It certainly shifted the attention to her — and off everyone and everything else.

In fact, if he ever got Teresa to change her mind on something in front of the group, she would suddenly become all smiles and say something like "Well, you've convinced me. Let's do it." This would quickly enlist the whole group.

Bill shook his head as he pondered. He had come to hate and dread meetings whenever he knew she would be in attendance.

He didn't like to think badly about people, but Teresa was just so difficult. On the occasions when she made the proposals, she would act as if everyone had an equal say but go on the attack if anyone ever actually disagreed with her.

As a follower, she was quick to question, debate, argue, and criticize, but as a manager, she wouldn't allow her team to do any of those things. She was an adamant authoritarian, quickly escalating from "Who has any questions?" to "You're wrong, so be quiet!" to "If you don't stop arguing with this proposal, you're going to be fired before you leave this room!"

After witnessing this even once or twice, those who worked with her pretty much never again had anything to say to the group. Everyone walked on eggshells whenever Teresa was near.

Yet she could be really great and effective at doing hard jobs, as long as she got her way. But honestly! It was like she was trying to make it hard for the group to accomplish anything! Like she was deliberately manipulating things so they'd go in circles until they missed out on every opportunity and finally just turned all the decisions over to her.

Bill, as the head of their group, was responsible for making their work effective and profitable, yet every time anyone tried to *go anywhere or accomplish anything, Teresa was there with her brilliant words forcing them to start over at ground zero.*

Should he fire her?

Did he need to think of some never-ending, self-contained assignment to get her distracted from everything else? He looked around the room again and saw the good people she had brought on board and the way she had influenced many at the table.

No, he didn't want to lose her. Somehow, with everything she did to disrupt the flow and cohesion of the group, she was also frequently amazing and unifying! She was a talented analyst and a brilliant marketer. Somehow, after everything, he needed her.

He just had to figure out a way to help her not be so difficult and annoying!

My Way or My Way

The Autocrat is an interesting type of person. To begin with, she is usually half rebel and half tyrant. It's a fascinating mix really. Very Machiavellian. When the Autocrat isn't in charge, she is all rebel.

But she is not the good kind of rebel who sees a need in society and fights for it. The good kind of rebel is what author Malcolm Gladwell calls an "Outlier"[1] or what author Chris Brady calls a "Rascal."[2] She is like Robin Hood, a thorn in the bad guy's side — taking on the abusive Establishment to help the little guy and stand for goodness and truth.

But the good kind of rebel is usually not difficult in person. In fact, she is almost always the opposite; she faces down Goliath because she cares about people and wants to help them.

The Autocratic rebel is another matter entirely. This person is a rebel mainly because she's a frustrated tyrant. She wants to be in charge, and until she is, she does whatever she can to weaken and undermine whoever *is* in charge.

Agendas within Agendas

This is a wholly negative attitude. The rebel part of the Autocrat is the teenager who won't synergize with the needs, goals, and vision of the family—who goes out of her way to make things difficult and cast doubt on every relationship. She's the person at work who argues with everything the leader says or proposes, without having a valid point or reason for coming forward except to put in her two cents and make it clear she isn't owned.

Or sometimes her hidden agenda is to lift her own status and tear down others. She's the fish who swims upstream, not because she's trying to pay the price to get somewhere that matters but just because she wants to make it harder for the other fish to get where they're going. And of course she's the child who doesn't like chocolate because "everyone does" and therefore convinces the crowd to pick on the kid who does like chocolate.

When the Autocrat is put in charge, she rules like a tyrant. She wants to control everything and everyone. She bullies and terrorizes, threatens and punishes. She turns awards and recognition into a show of her authority and power.

The Autocrat is characterized by contrariness and an attitude of "I'm in control" and will generally fight against even the *right* decisions and direction, just because someone else thought of them or others are already carrying them out. She is a rebel for rebellion's sake, not for the sake of meaningful resistance or a significant cause. She is a rebel because she's seeking power, and she is a tyrant for the sake of keeping and expanding her power.

To the Autocrat, it's more important to be original, independent, liberated, and especially in charge than to be in the right, do something truly meaningful, or earn genuine success in life.

Like Simon Legree in *Uncle Tom's Cabin*[3] or the White Witch in C. S. Lewis's *The Chronicles of Narnia*[4] series, the Autocrat loves to declare her independence, title, and power and make them known and felt by everyone, and she often does so at the expense of what actually matters in the situation. She certainly isn't looking out for other people.

While it can be great to be independent-minded and stand up for what you believe, even when others disagree, the Autocrat values this trait only in herself. She constantly attacks independence, creativity, or innovation in others.

This is clearly not the right kind of attitude for true leaders, and it firmly places the Autocrat in the realm of difficult people.

In fact, the Autocrat often favors the use of anger, manipulation, loud argument, combativeness, threats, and intimidation. She can be the most difficult of difficult people simply because she sees these behaviors as strengths and is committed to developing her ability to put them to use — while other people are trying to overcome these "bad habits," "temptations," and "weaknesses" in their lives. The Autocrat sees these as skills and tools and signs of her courage, not character flaws.

Not You = Right

The mentality of the Autocrat goes something like "I'm right because I'm me" or "I'm right because you're wrong" or sometimes even "I'm right because I'm not you or that other guy or anyone else." Rather than being dedicated to truth and right and fighting for them at all costs, she takes the stance of fighting *against* things at all costs, all the while claiming that she is merely fighting for justice and the truth.

Synergy, group vision, the authority of others, and any perceived danger to her own authority are primary targets for the Autocrat.

She isn't the person who stands so strongly for something that she steps on toes; she's the person who kicks so passionately for her cause or agenda that she breaks kneecaps. Plus, she kind of likes it. It's a bit fun for her.

The Autocrat is basically the opposite of the Bureaucrat, except that they're both extremely difficult people. The Autocrat has gone so far to the other extreme from the Bureaucrat that, instead of thinking life is all about following the rules and doing what others think ought to be done, she thinks life is about who sets the rules. And she wants to be the one.

If she is part of a system that has found a good and synergistic balance of progress and traditionalism, she decides it's about *dis*obeying the rules and scoffing at traditionalism *just* because too many people adhere to them—and because she hopes this will win her followers.

The Autocrat has adopted (sometimes unconsciously) a true principle as her inner mantra: Truth isn't a democracy. She understands there's something wrong with the Bureaucrat's narrow refusal to think outside the box. But in all this, she's missed an important point: Truth *really* isn't a democracy. While the mere fact that others—even *lots* of others—believe or do something doesn't make it true, it also doesn't make it false!

The Autocrat has difficulty understanding the whole picture and has contented herself with rebelling against the Bureaucrat, the Boss, the system, and pretty much everyone else—right up until she takes charge. At this point, ironically, she supports her status with an army of Bureaucrats all enforcing the rules on others.

As long as the Bureaucrats obey the Autocrat's first rule—that they must do what the Autocrat says without question and make others do the same—they get along admirably.

Good Rebel / Bad Rebel

Some Autocrats are actually extremely competent and truly great people to have on the team — if leaders can learn to bring them into a synergistic place where they work *with* and *for* the team instead of following their general tendency to compete with its purpose and energy.

Because she is so bold and courageous and isn't afraid to stand out or receive criticism and opposition, the Autocrat who has been brought into her best place in the team, the one most suited to her strengths and weaknesses, can be a huge asset to the cause and a great person to have on your side. An Autocrat who's genuinely been turned into a team player can be a fantastic ally and a powerful crusader against enemies and opposition — and for all positive progress.

Naturally, there are other less capable Autocrats who really are just interested in causing trouble until they get the power, but leaders who learn to effectively deal with them can minimize their damage and sometimes even help them find a meaningful and effective place in the workings of the group.

In the absence of good leadership, Autocrats can wreak havoc in the lives of everyone around them.

Mirror Workshop

Have you read the book *Rascal*[5] by Chris Brady? If so, review your notes in the book and ponder why a true Rascal can never be an Autocrat. If you haven't read *Rascal*, get a copy and read chapters two and three right away.

CHAPTER 6

The Bungee Jumper

No man is infallible.
— ENGLISH PROVERB

Carol was about to end the meeting without filling the position — she could always pick someone herself and assign that person to finalize the last details for the morning of the event; asking for a volunteer was just in case — when a hand went up. Just what she had worried about: Mike was volunteering for the project.

"Are you sure it won't be any trouble for you to be there that early and to handle things with the client?" Carol asked. It wasn't like Mike to rethink his choice, but there was always a chance he'd change his mind if pushed.

Or not.

As usual, he was enthusiastic about doing it, "absolutely certain" he could do a great job, and very clear that they could all "count on him."

This last part was exactly what Carol wasn't sure about. She could remember a few times when Mike had actually come through with what he had agreed to, but more often, he simply didn't. He was always apologetic — or had the perfect excuse. But he still let them down, and they had to figure out how to get things done at the last minute when he didn't come through.

Carol didn't consider herself harsh, but she probably would have fired someone else by now. Unfortunately, Mike was technically her partner, not her employee or part of her staff.

Between that and the benefits he did bring to the team, firing him was simply not an option. And for the same reasons, she couldn't even exactly say no. She'd tried that before, and Mike had been so convinced he was the best one for the job that he actually went and took the other guy off the project, only to drop the ball in the end.

Yet here he was again, telling everyone he'd take this one, no worries. And then he sent everyone home.

"What can I do about this situation?" Carol felt powerless and increasingly discouraged. "What do you do with a Mike?" she asked herself.

What indeed?

Yes, Yes, Yes, No

This type of difficult person is a special character. The Bungee Jumper is almost always a fairly capable and even helpful person, but he's still very much a "difficult person" because of the problems his inevitable scrapes will cause.

This is the guy who's so confident in his own abilities that he's always getting into huge trouble and needing someone to bail him out. He's the guy who doesn't ask for help until it's way too late because he's sure he'll be able to figure it out. He's also the guy who'll consistently put himself in harm's way because he thinks the harm can't touch or affect him.

As his name suggests, the Bungee Jumper willingly jumps off the cliff without taking the *whole* list of consequences into consideration. Sure, he knows his rope will catch him, but he forgets that at some point, he's going to want to come back up the cliff. For that, he'll be calling you at midnight while he hangs there in the canyon—six hours up a dirt road. Oh, and it won't even cross his mind that you have a big presentation to the board tomorrow morning at eight o'clock.

The Bungee Jumper is characterized by reckless confidence and enthusiasm, strongly tainted with a naïve belief that he—and everyone else around him—is bulletproof.

Like Lois Lane from the Superman[1] stories or Lydia Bennet in *Pride and Prejudice,*[2] the Bungee Jumper thinks he can do anything and handle any challenge without any help, which leads him to overcommit and cause all sorts of trouble when he can't follow through.

Then, after costing his loved ones Herculean efforts to rescue him, he has the audacity to think it was all wonderful—never realizing the toll his careless choices take.

I Think I Can!

For the Bungee Jumper, there's never a question of whether he can accomplish the tasks he agrees to, commits to, or decides to do. He's that sure of himself! Unfortunately, he tends to overcommit and undercommunicate about his plans, conflicts, limitations, and failures.

Sometimes, he won't tell anyone even after he realizes he's bitten off more than he can chew, and he lets the situation deteriorate even further, frequently to the point of failure.

He usually really does think he can handle the tasks he promises to do, and he genuinely intends to follow through on his commitments. But he lacks judgment and doesn't think about the details. In fact, sometimes he picks something else to do at the last minute, so his commitments are often broken as easily and with as little responsibility as they are made. His promises are quickly forgotten and often replaced with something of greater interest to him in the moment.

To repeat: He doesn't just forget things, though he does that, too. Many times, he just plain decides to blow off a commitment and do something else instead — regardless of whom he hurts or how deeply.

The Bungee Jumper means well and thinks he is off to conquer the world. But when a better offer comes up, or the project he's working on proves to be too hard or tedious for him, he either gives up easily without letting anyone know he's dropping the ball or keeps trying when he really should be asking for advice or assistance. He leaves others holding the bag more often than he actually fulfills a commitment.

Thus, his dedication usually feels strong but is more often flaky and unreliable, and his communication is even worse. Because of this, people often feel betrayed or let down by the Bungee Jumper who promised to perform or show up and simply didn't.

Just Jump!

There are two main types of Bungee Jumpers: (1) those who give up too soon and (2) those who don't ask for help when they should. The ones who fit into the second type tend to be way more helpful in general because you can always count on them to do their best to fulfill their promises and accomplish what they say they will. The difficulty is that they don't anticipate problems or potential snags in their approach, and they usually don't recognize or communicate when they need help.

What is good about these Bungee Jumpers in the second category is that they're excited to plunge into new endeavors, and they usually try their best to make things work out. Leaders who effectively open and monitor the channels of communication with them and send in backup when needed will find these high-functioning Bungee Jumpers to be some of the most dedicated and passionate players on the team, as well as great catalysts at the beginning of projects.

The first type of Bungee Jumper, the kind that gives up too easily without letting anyone know and quickly jumps off the next cliff — and the next and the next — is much more difficult to work with and tends to be very difficult to rely on or trust with important tasks or responsibilities. This kind of person, one who has trouble *following through,* will always have trouble developing a *following.*

Mirror Workshop

Is your word your bond? When you say you'll do something, do you always come through (or communicate quickly and make things right if circumstances change)? If you're not sure, ask your mentor.

Making this one character change — to being a person of firm integrity, fully trustworthy — in yourself if needed is a vital step to becoming a real leader.

Top leaders walk their talk. Period.

CHAPTER 7

The Politician (and the Critic)

Story is honorable and trustworthy;
plot is shifty, and best kept under house arrest.
—STEPHEN KING

The two women watched as Lacy walked out to her car. As soon as the door was shut, Miranda turned to Ashley, and the torrent began.

Sometimes Ashley was surprised at how nice Miranda could seem when they were all together, given how much she appeared to hate Lacy. Still, at least she wasn't chasing Lacy around with all of her issues, confronting her and bossing her. Or maybe that wasn't such a good thing.

Sometimes Miranda's concerns seemed totally legitimate. Ashley didn't think Lacy was a bad person by any means, but she did sometimes do or say things that hurt Miranda's feelings. After all, nobody's perfect! So it wasn't like Miranda was always wrong and Lacy was always right.

In fact, sometimes Ashley left their weekly meetings thinking what was really needed was a good, sincere apology from Lacy. She could certainly be a little blunt. But what was Ashley supposed to do about it? She couldn't exactly fix the problem for the two women; it had nothing to do with her! Whenever Miranda talked about her issues with Lacy, she was talking to all the people who couldn't fix them.

This went on for years. Then one morning, everything changed. Ashley had to leave early, and when she got to the car, she realized she had left her keys in the house. When she returned to the front porch, she heard Miranda talking to Lacy.

At first, Ashley was surprised that Miranda would say such things directly to Lacy's face — especially in such hateful tones and words.

Then suddenly, Ashley realized something. Miranda wasn't talking about Lacy. She was talking about her!

Ashley found it hard to breathe as she processed this new realization. "All these years that she's been gossiping to me about Lacy, she has been doing the same with Lacy about me. She's been acting nice to my face and then attacking me behind my back!"

Flattery Never Faileth?

Don't let the root word *polite* in the Politician's name fool you, let alone the apparent politeness in her treatment of you. Gentility is not always a sign of character; sometimes it is a screen for a lack thereof. In many ways, the Politician is the most difficult of difficult people because she never directly confronts you with her issues. Like the classic, stereotypical idea of a "nasty politician," she prefers to spread all her difficulty behind your back, in backroom deals and behind-the-scenes maneuvering.

The Politician is the passive-aggressive wife who instead of working things out or even fighting with her husband spreads all sorts of nasty rumors about him at her weekly moms group or monthly book club. She's the sweet-faced coworker who smiles and smirks to your face and then stabs you in the back when you're not looking. And she's the "ever-loyal" second in command who's secretly plotting to overthrow her leader, usurp his position, and leave him to rot in prison.

The Politician is characterized by her persona of goodwill and friendship when you *are* looking and her gossiping, triangulation, and enemy status as soon as you're *not*.

Like Caroline Bingley from Jane Austen's *Pride and Prejudice*,[1] Gríma Wormtongue from J. R. R. Tolkien's *The Lord of the Rings*,[2] or the "popular girl" from pretty much any movie about high school, the Politician thinks it's her job to be on good terms with everybody in person and yet to always follow their exit with an in-depth, ruthless, and biting critique of what makes them a total failure at life — all as part of her secret agenda to rise in personal power, reputation, or situation.

As a result, she tends to be a notorious gossip, a shameless and two-faced schemer, and a passive-aggressive tattletale. The Politician is certainly a difficult person, and almost everyone will eventually encounter one or more such people in life.

Right Where I Want You!

Again, the Politician usually seems harmless and even friendly in person. But either she's too scared to address problems head on with the people involved, or else doing so doesn't suit her plan to make them pay. In either case, you're usually the last person to find out she has a problem with you, even though she's probably confided in you often about *other* people's issues and shortcomings.

She can be easily spotted by the way she waits until someone leaves to tell her "real friends" what makes the other person a loser. And chances are if she's willing to talk to you about someone else, she'll do the same with others about you.

In some ways, the Politician is the opposite of the Boss. Instead of being in your face about stuff that is none of her business, she attacks you when you can't defend yourself. And she's often relentless.

The Critic

There is even a special subcategory of the Politician called the Critic, who seems to think it is his life purpose to criticize, disparage, and spread rumors about others. The Critic often does this even if he's never met the person he criticizes. He decides to harp on and vilify whoever his current chosen target is, and when he doesn't get enough people supporting him in his scorn, he just starts making up lies about the person or group he's criticizing.

This kind of difficult person fits the Politician model because he doesn't seem to have the courage to deal with a person directly. He just snipes and spreads half-truths, innuendo, and downright fabrications from the safety of distance or anonymity.

Needless to say, this can be a very difficult kind of person to deal with. He usually won't listen to reason or even facts—because he is so sure he is right and you are wrong that the "facts" for him are whatever he most strongly feels they are. But even with the Critic, the Five-Step Peace Process is extremely effective, as we will find out in part two.

What to Expect

The Politician, including the Critic, seldom comes directly to you with a concern when she has something she legitimately ought to discuss with you. Sadly, this lack of conversation isn't because she's so willing to forgive and move on that she never needs a confrontation. Quite the contrary.

The Politician certainly has problems with others that she's not ready to forgive, but rather than pursuing a real solution and resolution with the person in question, she prefers to debrief the matter with everyone else—and maybe, while she's at it, think of a few sneaky ways to exact revenge and come out on top.

Someone who gossips and triangulates behind another person's back is almost always a Politician to some degree, and it's a good idea to pay attention and note such behavior; it's very seldom a one-time occurrence. More often, it represents a settled habit or even a strongly developed personality trait—one that's bound to come out at the worst times and in ways that pose a danger to individual relationships and overall group effectiveness.

In short, if a person is being the Politician with you, she almost certainly does the same thing with others—now or in the past. Remember, what a Politician will do *with* you, she'll do *to* you!

More or Less

In some cases, Politicians are not so much conniving schemers as people with a skewed worldview and a few bad habits. In such cases, leaders can be a great influence on them and help them learn to be more direct, honest, and courageous in their concerns and difficulties rather than continuing to take the gossiping and criticizing route.

As would-be Politicians develop some courage and an understanding of how to honestly and directly deal with people and problems, they can become upstanding members of your group and of society—but only if they are willing to take action and change.

In these cases, while a passive-aggressive gossiper is still extremely difficult to deal with, the problem is really not so deep or impossible to solve as it is in the further-gone cases. This type of Politician simply needs the right information and some help and support in developing the courage to fully apply and use good relationship principles.

In the case of the other Politicians, the ones who are really out to get someone, it's much more difficult. This actually makes it even more important for leaders to learn to effectively deal with such cases. These are the people who will cause deep and lasting trouble in a family, company, organization, neighborhood, community, or group when they're left unrecognized and unchecked.

That said, learning to effectively deal with Politicians — both the weak and the malicious types — is an important part of good leadership and will bring the team more top performers and valuable members. Good leadership of this kind can be invaluable in helping your group sidestep big problems and potentially dangerous internal enemies, as they realize they'll be protected from passive-aggressive back-channeling by a leader and culture that will not allow it.

Mirror Workshop

Stephen Covey spoke about the importance of having integrity toward people who aren't present. Never gossip. If you must be critical, do so honestly and directly to the person's face.

Create a habit of avoiding gossip. Period. If you ever find yourself gossiping or listening to gossip, train yourself to stop, change the subject, and move on — or leave.

Gossip never helped anyone, and it has hurt a lot of people—especially those who do the gossiping.

When the gossip pertains to a public figure, such as a celebrity or well-known political personality, the same principle applies. It's okay to disagree with ideas, but attacking another person is almost always weak and cowardly.

Also, nearly all gossip about public figures is wildly inaccurate. A wise leader once taught that if you really want to know about a person, ask his friends, not his enemies. Friends typically feel the need to exercise fairness and impartiality rather than just sugarcoating what they say about their close friends. In contrast, enemies usually feel the need to exaggerate the flaws, ignore the strengths, and just plain twist the truth about those they are attacking.

This rule of thumb nearly always holds true: Friends will try to be fair and, thus, give you the truth, while enemies will try to be extreme. It's rare to ever find enemies who try to be fair or friends who gush with nice lies. It just doesn't happen much.

On a personal level, "no gossip at all" is the rule of top leaders. Top leaders don't make it to where they are without on occasion being misquoted, criticized, lied about, or unfairly attacked, so they know that the value of gossip is exactly zero. Actually, it's a negative value, since it can cause damage.

To become a top leader, follow their rule: no gossip, anywhere, anytime, for any reason. And do not trust those who engage in gossip or cowardly criticism—the Politicians—because they have an agenda and a very bad habit.

Conclusion

There are other kinds of difficult people in the world beyond the seven main types mentioned here in part one. No doubt you can think of various difficult people in your life experience who don't quite match any of these categories.

Whether or not a difficult person fits one of the profiles we have provided, the real question is how to effectively deal with difficult people, and for that purpose, these seven broad categories will prove to be quite helpful.

We will now turn our attention to the Five-Step Peace Process, which will give you an excellent basis for dealing with difficult people effectively and successfully.

PART TWO

The Five-Step
Peace Process

*Part one can be summed up in two ways. First, don't
be a difficult person. Don't be any of the seven main types
of difficult people, and don't be difficult in any other way
either. Top leaders learn that being difficult simply isn't
part of the path to effective leadership.*

*Second, know the main types of difficult people because
it can help you empathize with — and respond to — those
who struggle. Being difficult holds people back, and as a
leader, you can help many overcome this hurdle to their
success.*

*The way to deal with difficult people — effectively,
successfully, and consistently — is to apply the principles
of the Five-Step Peace Process. Understanding this process
is important for leaders who hope to accomplish anything
big and meaningful. As Sun Tzu said, "If in the midst of
difficulties we are always ready to seize an advantage, we
may extricate ourselves from misfortune."[1]*

The bottom line is this: Part of leadership is dealing well with difficult people. Some difficult people are just a few steps away from being top performers and excellent allies, and good leaders can help them succeed. There are also difficult people who plan on staying difficult and even specifically trying to hurt you and your goals, and leaders must know how to effectively deal with them as well.

The Five-Step Peace Process works, whether you're dealing with well-meaning difficult people who want to change or those with a more reluctant or even malicious intent. Without the principles of this process, few of us will successfully deal with the difficult people we will inevitably encounter. This process is powerful and effective.

PEACE stands for:
Pause (Step 1)
Empathy (Step 2)
Agility (Step 3)
Contribution (Step 4)
Epiphany (Step 5)

STEP 1

Pause

Human freedom involves our capacity to pause between the stimulus and response and, in that pause, to choose the one response toward which we wish to throw our weight. The capacity to create ourselves, based upon this freedom, is inseparable from consciousness or self-awareness.

—ROLLO MAY

CHAPTER 8

The Power of Pause

Evaluating the benefits and drawbacks of
any relationship is your *responsibility. You do*
not have to passively accept what is brought
to you. You can choose.
—DEBORAH DAY, M. A.

There is a real and fundamental disconnect between the way people naturally and reflexively tend to react to difficult situations and people and the way top leaders approach comparable circumstances.

In other words, top leaders handle difficult situations, particularly difficult people, in a way that is profoundly different from the norm. This often makes the difference between success and failure in handling these encounters,

> *Top leaders handle difficult situations, particularly difficult people, in a way that is profoundly different from the norm.*

since the reflex to respond *to* difficulty *with* difficulty generally produces bad results. The natural, knee-jerk response to difficult people is usually less effective than following the right approach.

Yet, interestingly enough, top leaders are not exempt from the instinctual "fight or flight" reflex to run away, respond in kind, yell back harder, resort to a power struggle, or become any of the types of difficult people themselves. Fighting fire with fire is the first thought for most people—even top leaders. They have no magical or ethereal immunity.

So what makes the difference?

Stimulus____Response

Psychologist and Holocaust survivor Viktor Frankl said, "Between stimulus and response, there is a space. In that space is our power to choose our response. In our response lies our growth and our freedom."[1]

He also famously taught that this ability to choose our response, regardless of the difficulty of the situation or environment, is something that no one can ever take from us. It is innately and inalienably ours. Human beings, and not just the special race of "top leaders," have the power to *choose* how they will respond, even to the most difficult people and circumstances.

The fact that this principle was widely taught by a survivor of Nazi concentration camps is significant. This man dealt with the difficult guards and prisoners in what could easily be termed *extremely* difficult circumstances.

Despite having to deal with highly difficult people in such an environment, he understood this important principle and the responsibility that comes with this innately human trait. We choose before we act, even when we are first acted upon.

It is in how top leaders use this trait or ability — or perhaps more particularly this *space* in which decisions are made — that they often differ from less effective and less successful counterparts.

The power of this space is legendary and very real. One thought-provoking term for the space between stimulus and response is simply "Pause."

P Is for Pause

In his book *The Pause Principle,* author Kevin Cashman calls "Pause" one of the most powerful tools in the human world. It is also the first vital step to dealing with difficult people and the *P* in the Five-Step Peace Process.

Cashman said, "Pause, the natural capability to step back in order to move forward with greater clarity, momentum, and impact, holds the creative power to reframe and refresh how we see ourselves and our relationships, our challenges, our capacities, our organizations and missions within a larger context."[2]

While this space technically exists in every situation where human beings are involved, the length of the pause and the level of consciousness with which it is attended vary extensively. What leaders do that many others don't is as simple as turning this natural space into a conscious and intentional pause. This seemingly small detail makes the difference in their ability to properly and effectively deal with difficult people.

Unless we use this space and pause well, we will not deal well with difficult people.

When we draw the pause out long enough, we can fill it with the right kind of thinking, observing, questioning, and therefore understanding. This turns a reflexive but hardly noticeable "space" into a fully formed, well-timed, and completely utilized choice. In doing this, we ensure that the actions we choose are based on deliberation and thought.

> *By making a point of actively and purposefully choosing, we increase our likelihood of choosing well.*

In short, by making a point of actively and purposefully choosing, we increase our likelihood of choosing well, not to mention the conviction with which we then stand behind our choice once it has been made and acted upon.

Flip the Forces and Get It Right!

Kevin Cashman cited Bob Johansen, author of *Leaders Make the Future*, who described what he called the "VUCA" world: a world that is "Volatile, Unpredictable, Complex, and Ambiguous." This perfectly describes the world we face whenever we deal with difficult people. Johansen said that the goal of leaders must be to "flip the VUCA forces to terms that create possibilities and redefine VUCA as: Vision; Understanding; Clarity; and Agility."

This statement elegantly describes leadership, and this reversal, as Cashman taught, is the purpose of the Pause.[3]

Imagine that you are confronted, right now, by a difficult person. He may be a Boss, a Politician, an Autocrat, or a Diva. Or he might just be angry, loud, and bent on chewing you out or berating your business partner or spouse.

Whatever the situation, the first step isn't to react. It is to Pause. This can be done in milliseconds in your mind, but it is vital.

As you take a mental step outside the situation, use the natural space provided between stimulus and response, and choose to reframe your circumstances in a responsible and leadership-minded way, you are breaking the cycle of conflict caused by the difficult person. This is what top leaders do, and it makes all the difference.

This break alone is worth the Pause. But it gets even better. As you Pause, you break your own emotions from the angry, frustrated, or stressful energy coming from the difficult person, and this prepares you to deal with him in a different way than the manner in which he is approaching you. Just as when the connection of a battery is broken, Pause takes you out of the difficulty for a few seconds. This alters your perception drastically. When the difficulty is gone from your mind, all that is left is the person. You don't see him as a difficulty but simply as a fellow human. This changes everything.

Pause also reminds you that *you* are a human and that you need to deal with the situation as an excellent person, not a difficult one. Pause is powerful, and you can easily make it a habit. More on this later.

During this Pause, think about what lasting results you want when the conversation with the difficult person is over. Consider the kind of results that naturally come from following the right process, taking the right steps, and allowing yourself to Pause and make the right choices.

The Difficult Person in Front of You

Next, quickly identify what type of difficult person you are dealing with. Is he acting like the Politician? You'll need to get him talking to you directly — instead of making nice and then attacking you from the shadows.

But if he is choosing to be the Boss, you'll want do the opposite. Get him to write down his suggestions and submit them in bullet format so you can benefit from them.

If he's playing the Autocrat, schedule a meeting for later. Talk to him when you can deal with the issues face to face and one on one and get him aligned with the team's goals in a way that benefits everyone and helps him get what he really wants by helping others with what they need from him.

If the difficult person is being a Diva, schedule a meeting for later, just as with the Autocrat. But instead of alignment, focus on making a detailed plan that you can both agree on — one that gives certain perks for specific accomplishments. The Diva is actually one of the easiest to deal with because of his strong desire for perks and special treatment. Work out an agreement where he'll get

just what he wants in return for his prespecified perfor-
mance. Then be sure you always deliver what you promised — immediately when he meets the agreed upon goals.

If he's the Bungee Jumper, you've got time to deal with
the situation because he won't seem difficult at first. Just
make sure you put a good support mechanism in place to
help him follow through on whatever he promises.

If the difficult person you encounter is the Victim,
find a way to mentor him or get him an attentive mentor
who will point out his specific blind spots and help him
work on them — in a spirit of support, love, and firmness.
Mentoring is extremely effective for the Victim, if it is done
well and with high consistency.

If he is being the Bureaucrat and you are his superior,
just remind him of this and tell him what to do. If you
aren't his official superior, you have three choices.

The first option is to make it clear that you are somehow
above him in the pecking order with which he views life.
This can be difficult, since he won't take your word for it
and will want verification from his own boss.

The second is to show him that you are not subject to
his jurisdiction and then walk away and do whatever
you want. This puts the ball in his court to do the work of
coming after you to show you that you are under his jurisdiction, which he may or may not decide to do.

The third option is to smile, put up with his rules and
difficulty, and get on with more important matters in your
life (which is what the majority of people do most of the
time).

Any of the three might be right, depending on the situation.

If you do not engage your own Pause with the Bureaucrat, you might spend a lot of wasted energy and resources on options one and two. If you do choose Pause, you'll see him as a human and yourself as an excellent leader. This combination will help you make the best decisions, even when dealing with a difficult person.

Don't Skip Your Power

Deal with different kinds of difficult people in the way best suited to get the results you want. The key to this is Pause. Without Pause, you'll hardly ever be wise in such a situation.

This bears repeating: You're going to deal with each type of difficult person differently — as best suited to the unique wants and needs of each. There is no set plan for dealing with each type because every person is unique, but Pause will give you the power to deal successfully in all situations.

But this all hinges on a good Pause. Otherwise, if you're like most people, you'll usually respond emotionally and lose the chance to lead, control the situation for the good of the group, improve the personal relationship, and encourage the best results.

This may feel like a tall order, and without the Pause, it's practically impossible. But with Pause, it's surprisingly easy. It really is.

Again, this can happen very quickly—as rapidly as thought. But it makes a huge, lasting difference. Instead of letting the difficult person control you with his emotions, rage, or other passions, you step back and take control of the situation. By controlling yourself, as Sun Tzu taught, you take charge of the whole interaction.

This may seem simple or even too easy. But it is very real, and it works. As you learn and master this first step, you'll be much closer to achieving the other steps more effectively, since Steps 2 through 5 depend on taking this first one and getting it right. Pause makes the whole process work.

In fact, Step 1 gets you almost halfway there, and until you Pause, you'll likely never be able to deal with difficult people in the best way.

Learn this vital skill. Use your ability to choose your response, and don't be afraid to Pause before you act! In fact, learn to Pause whenever any difficulty arises. When you are confronted by a difficult person or situation, immediately Pause. Pause is power.

CHAPTER 9

The Power of Pause Applied to You: Don't Be That Person

We practice mastering ourselves in the moment so that we can better open ourselves to being a servant leader and to harness our emotions and choose what to do with our reactions.
— LYSSA ADKINS

In learning the other steps of the Five-Step Peace Process, you'll inevitably learn how to best fill your Pause time, but before we can really move beyond this point, there are some important ideas that require further inspection.

First, fix you. You may not consider yourself a difficult person, but everyone has the potential to be difficult given the right situation, mood, and people. For example, a person who would never get angry when confronted by the Boss or the Bungee Jumper may find herself very upset when she spends a lot of time with the Victim or the Autocrat.

Alternatively, you may not get emotional the first time you deal with the Victim, or even the first twenty times, but at some point, your frustration may suddenly (and even surprisingly) rise to the surface. You may just get tired of coping and snap.

Different people are triggered emotionally by different things, and almost everyone has the potential to be a difficult person under certain circumstances. The power of Pause gives you control over every situation, regardless of the circumstances. If you learn to master your Pause button, you will always be in charge. If not, your emotions may sometimes surprise you.

For example, imagine you are confronted by a person playing the Autocrat or the Bungee Jumper, and you are a bit frustrated but don't think you need a real Pause this time. You decide to give the person a little advice, and you're sure she'll just listen without difficulty. Even if you are right, you have a problem.

By skipping the Pause, you glossed over the reality that the Autocrat and the Bungee Jumper seldom respond to advice. They tend to think your advice applies to someone else, not them. (Same with the Victim.) Whatever you say, you're probably wasting your time.

If you Pause, however, you naturally ask yourself: "How do I want this to turn out? Who am I dealing with? What are this person's weaknesses, strengths, and constraints? Given these realities, what's the best way to proceed?"

This can happen quickly, or you can take a little time and get back with the person when you've thought it through. Either way, the Pause gives you power—power that is always lost if you skip your Pause. It's important not to move straight from the stimulus to response without giving Pause the weight and process it requires.

So what makes an effective Pause?

What's *Your* Inner Difficult Person?

Unfortunately, as mentioned, even the best leaders in the world have a difficult person lurking somewhere inside them, waiting to be released in a moment of low self-control or high personal weakness. The difference between a top leader and the difficult person himself is not in a fundamental separation of natural tendencies but in the leader's resolve to control those inner tendencies and the mastery he achieves in doing so.

To put it simply, top leaders recognize the existence of difficult people—even when those difficulties are within themselves—and they take the steps necessary to understand the best ways to deal with different types of difficult people and situations. Moreover, they take responsibility for dealing with them in the best possible ways.

The first thing to do in Pause mode, then, is identify your own type of inner difficulty and take the steps necessary to counteract it in yourself. Ask yourself: "Which of the seven main types (or other types) of difficult people is rising in me right now?"

Once you answer this question, immediately take control. If your inner Boss shows up, avoid the temptation to start lecturing. If your inner Victim comes, don't start whining or blaming. If your inner Autocrat is trying to speak, don't start throwing around your title, power, or threats of reprisal.

If your inner Bungee Jumper arrives, don't just smile and make whatever promises will defuse the situation. If your inner Politician shows up, don't just make nice and smooth everything over, only to later make sure you tell people what a loser this difficult person you are dealing with really is. The list goes on.

Whatever you are tempted to do that isn't your inner top leader, don't do it. Control yourself. This is the first part of Pause. You break the connection to negativity and knee-jerk responses, and you take control of your own inner difficult person that is trying to come out and sabotage you.

So to reiterate, Step 1 starts with two things. First, control your own difficult self. In his speech "Dealing with Difficult People," bestselling author Chris Brady teaches that the number-one thing to do in dealing with difficult people is to *not* be one yourself, since, as top leader Tim Marks puts it, "Everywhere you go, there you are!"[1]

People who contribute to the problem of a difficult person by being difficult themselves have missed the whole point of Pause, and they are likely to cause extra trouble for whoever happens to be the *real* leader in the room.

Second, use the Pause to ask yourself what type of difficult person you are dealing with, and respond accordingly. This is simple, yet powerful.

Check Your Own Nose!

Brady shared a story about a father who one day when changing his baby's diaper inadvertently scratched his nose before washing his hands. Alas! Without noticing, he left a trace of less-than-pleasant-smelling matter just inside his nose and went on with his day.

For the rest of the day, every time he walked into a room, he noticed a bad smell and became convinced that some child had had an accident there, that someone had left a diaper in the trash, or that some other such catastrophe had occurred.

Unfortunately, the man never thought to question whether he was at fault, and so he never really figured out what was going on. Everywhere the man went, he was sure that some big problem was causing the smell, when he was the one carrying it around himself![2]

Negative Synergy

The message here is clear: when facing a difficult person or situation, removing one potential difficulty (your own choice to be difficult) from the picture makes it much easier to come to a positive solution.

If both parties in the conversation are difficult people, there is almost no chance that one of them will miraculously achieve the perfect solution despite the synergy of difficultness. And on the rare occasion it does happen, it results from luck rather than any extraordinary insight, ability, or leadership on the part of difficult person number one (you).

The solution is quite simple. Pause! Take the natural prep time allotted you between stimulus and response and use it to choose some role other than your own inner difficult person.

Help Yourself

There is more. After understanding your general tendencies to be a difficult person sometimes, the next part of your effective Pause is to take into account the more specific factors that might tempt you to be difficult *today*. For example, if you've had an extremely emotional, stressful, or difficult day, you might be more likely to skip over the Five-Step Peace Process and head straight to an emotional response. In such cases, you'll rarely happen upon the best choices.

Taking time to remember and check not only general tendencies but also specific susceptibilities is an important part of Pause, as it allows leaders to take conscious control of the situation rather than being automatically and unduly influenced by outside forces, personal moods, environmental challenges, or the pressure of today's complications. To put it simply, when you are having a bad day, it is even harder to react coolly and correctly to any more difficulty. Recognizing this in the moment helps counteract the tendency to give in to the instinct to jump the gun in reaction.

Of course, it's important to note that the purpose of empathizing with yourself in these scenarios is *not* to help you excuse bad behavior or the wrong response by making it seem justifiable or "natural" but instead to help you recognize the factors that are influencing your decision *before* you actually act, so you have ample opportunity to choose wisely.

Majority ≠ Rule

Mark Twain could practically be famous just for his ability to say great things in obnoxious ways (actually, he is), but he made yet another excellent point when he said, "Whenever you find yourself on the side of the majority, it is time to reform—(or pause and reflect)."[3] This is a great reminder to anyone who hopes to become adept at dealing with difficult people.

As the majority of people tend to allow themselves to become difficult when faced with difficult people or circumstances, being on their side is really not the best option for those seeking to effectively lead. Twain's solution—to Pause and reflect—is exactly what is most needed in such situations.

So when you find yourself on the side of the difficult majority, Pause. Take stock of who you tend to be and what you feel like right now. Contrast these with who you ought to be and want to be. And then *choose* your character for the current interaction.

You are not an animal. Nor are you simply a member of a mob. You get to slough off your inner difficulty and be the leader you know you can be! This is one of the most important and powerful aspects of Pause. Take a moment to be the leader you really are, the one who is best suited to deal with the difficult person in front of you in an effective and compelling way.

As you pay the price to shed your own difficult ways and choose instead to be a genuinely excellent person and leader, a person who exemplifies the best qualities and traits, you'll tend to attract more of the same kind of people in your life, and you'll be ready for the difficult ones—who come, no matter how incredible you are.

This is the person you want to be, the person you *should* be. It's also the person who'll be best at working with all kinds of people and, ultimately, the person who's best suited to live your purpose and accomplish your dreams.

And on top of all that, it's the kind of person who's actually ready to effectively meet the challenge of dealing with difficult people. So Pause, reflect, and choose to stop being the difficult you and start being the real and best you.

You know you want to do this, and until you do, guess what? Your life will be absolutely *full* of difficult people— because everywhere you go, there you'll be!

CHAPTER 10

Opposition Happens; Pick Your Battles

Be yourself; everyone else is taken.
— UNKNOWN, OFTEN ATTRIBUTED TO OSCAR WILDE

Another important concept for leaders to consider during the Pause step is that opposition is natural in anything. It's simply a side effect of *doing*. That said, not every difficult person you encounter is one you need to worry about very much. Don't overreact.

Sometimes a good Pause is all it takes for top leaders to decide that the person in front of them isn't one they need to confront. In such cases, the "how to deal with them" becomes very simple: move on.

Those who hope to become top leaders will at some point find a cause or purpose that matters to them more than almost anything else. This is their "one true success," what they dedicate their life to supporting.

Sometimes Pause is the only step in the process of dealing with difficult people because during this step, the leader becomes aware that the potential battle or inter-action she's confronted with has very little importance in the context of her own personal mission or cause. In other words, in many cases, the Pause allows the leader to recognize those situations for which an escalation or confrontation is just not worthwhile.

When this is the answer, it's more important than ever that the leader in the situation actually understands the principle of Pause and uses it correctly to realign herself with who she is and what she stands for. If she omits the Pause step and takes action to deal with a difficult person when there is no need and nothing to be gained, she can cause distractions or even very serious problems—and some of them last and hurt for a long time.

Such distractions are usually unnecessary. It is important during Pause to decide when to move on versus when to hunker down, take on a difficult person, and engage.

> *If you don't have opposition in what you're doing, you either don't have a big enough purpose or you don't have enough courage to match your purpose.*

Opposition Happens!

Top leaders understand that learning to effectively and rightly deal with difficult people won't mean there's no opposition at all. In fact, they know that when a person doesn't have opposition, there's a bigger problem at work. If you don't have opposition in what you're doing, you either don't have a big enough purpose or you don't have enough courage to match your purpose.

If you are taking great action toward a great purpose, opposition will come. Sometimes the difficult people who come along are simply the proof that leaders are making a real difference. They're difficult in that they're opposition. In such cases, leaders learn to rejoice at such evidence that they're on the right track, without wasting too much time or energy trying to convince or appeal to all the naysayers.

As Albert Einstein reminded us, "Great spirits have always encountered violent opposition from mediocre minds."[1] When that's the kind of opposition or difficulty being offered, wise people don't give it more energy than it deserves because they Pause long enough to recognize it for what it is. This matters—a lot. Otherwise good leaders can get bogged down or stray off track very easily by trying to take on every difficult person even when it's just a waste.

This is another important part of a well-spent Pause. The people who are most successful at dealing with difficult people are the ones who use some of their Pause to consider whether dealing with this person helps or forwards their life purpose. If it doesn't, they find a way to move on without any further confrontation or difficulty. They let it go. This takes maturity, but it is vital for leaders.

What It's *Not* About

Frankly, learning to deal with difficult people is about successfully avoiding the ones who'll stand in your way and effectively serving and working with the ones who could help you reach new heights, given the right kind of attitude and leadership.

This is big. Wasting too much time or concern on any other kind of difficult person is usually immature and irresponsible. This is a powerful lesson that will make those who learn and apply it exponentially more effective in whatever they're trying to accomplish in the world.

Effectively dealing with difficult people isn't about pacifying or escaping the kind of opposition that comes from being an effective leader. It's about knowing when to ignore difficult people and how to engage those who shouldn't be ignored.

The Votes That Count

Pause is also a time to remember that life is not a popularity contest, and effectively dealing with difficult people does not mean you're running for an office where you have to get everyone to vote for you. In fact, even politicians who actually are trying to get people to vote for them understand that it's not about pleasing everyone. They know to look for the "swing" votes — in other words, the votes that actually count.

They know some people will support them no matter what they say, and others they'll never convince. So instead of spending all their time trying to influence, please, or change these two groups, they focus their energy on the swing voters—the ones they still hope to sway.

While not all swing voters can be accurately categorized as "difficult people," finding and swaying your swing voters is one of the main points of learning to deal with difficult people, and Pause is a great time to consider which category the difficult person in question falls under. Knowing this before ever moving to Step 2 is essential.

This may seem like it's about seeing who the other person is, which would make it part of Empathizing, but it's actually more about knowing who *you* are. This isn't about who the other person is or what he or she stands for. It's simply the part of Pause where you remember what *you* stand for.

Those who Pause to do this important regrouping in their minds will be better prepared for the next few steps in the process, and they'll also avoid a lot of unnecessary conflict and difficulty in life. Pause includes wisely picking your battles, rather than allowing them to pick you.

Pick Your Battles

Top leaders don't waste their time trying to satisfy the difficult people who are going to oppose them in anything they do that truly matters. That's like mud-wrestling with a pig. You'll probably never win, you'll both get all sorts of dirty, and the pig will enjoy the whole thing—not to mention beat you in experience every time.

Leaders pick their battles. They know that they're not looking to please everyone. And they use Pause to remind themselves of this and act accordingly.

As you keep this understanding in mind, you'll be far better at letting the insignificant problems go so you can focus on the ones that are worth your time. This is one of the reasons Pause matters so much!

When you actually Pause to reflect in the space between stimulus and response, you get the chance to decide if it's really worth it to respond in a way that leads to a confrontation or even any kind of interaction at all. When you don't Pause, the difficult person gets to decide his place in the running of your life and mission.

Understanding, remembering, and using this principle will make an enormous difference in your effectiveness at dealing with difficult people and, more important, at accomplishing whatever it is you've set out to do in your life.

If you don't know why you're fighting, you can never hope to win. In contrast, if you pick your battles based on your purpose, you'll be able to make them really count for something—something that matters!

CHAPTER 11

Pause; Don't Wait

The more Susan waited, the more the
doorbell didn't ring. Or the phone.
—DOUGLAS ADAMS

One final detail everyone needs to clearly understand about Pause is that it in no way excuses procrastination, letting wounds fester, or fiddling while Rome burns.

Pause is a principle of leadership and excellence, never something to hide behind in order to avoid difficult actions or leave necessary words unsaid. Understanding and remembering this is vitally important to success in any aspect of life, especially in dealing with difficult people.

While it is essential to take a moment to determine proper action, successful people know that it's also crucially important to take action at some point. They realize that the longer they wait to address a difficult person or situation, the more they risk becoming part of the difficulty themselves and the more likely it is that the whole thing will blow up in their faces.

Just Take the Shoe Off!

Imagine you have a tiny pebble in your shoe, and instead of getting it out right away, you leave it there and continue your day's ten-mile hike. By the time you get home, your foot naturally has some pretty bad blisters and hurts quite a lot. Unfortunately, you're afraid to get into it because it "might get messy," so you leave your shoe on as you go about your life.

It's a little uncomfortable to sleep, shower, and dress in hiking boots, but you're afraid to see what'll happen when you actually dig into it. Eventually, after days, nights, weeks, and even months with that little rock in there, you've got a festering wound that develops gangrene, and the doctor says you'll have to lose the entire foot. Clearly this is a lot worse than if you had taken a few seconds right at the beginning to dispose of the little rock when it was nothing more than a minor annoyance.

This example may seem like an overly simplified illustration of the principle because sometimes difficult situations start out a lot more uncomfortable to deal with than merely removing a pebble from a shoe. But when you consider that such situations also tend to have a fairly big margin of escalation, it becomes apparent that it's important to deal with them early—even when doing so seems harder than letting them go.

The solution, then, is simple. Don't wait! When the problem seems small, leaders know that it can get bigger, and they take steps to see that it doesn't. If the problem is small today, today is the best time to fix it. If it'll be uncomfortable to address a minor issue, imagine how uncomfortable it will be to address a huge one.

The Oak versus the Sprout

This is like the man who went to build his house on a lot that had a massive oak tree. For a while, he tried working around it, but at some point during construction, it became clear that the tree would have to go. The process of removing it was a major ordeal that took excessive time, energy, and money, and it made the whole construction process much harder for everyone involved.

As the man watched some workers digging out roots hour after hour, he imagined what a difference it would have made if he could have transported himself many years into the past to deal with the tree. "I could have literally plucked it from the ground with two fingers, roots and all," he said to himself.

This is often the case with difficult people. If they're handled correctly at the beginning, they're no more than a little sprout. But when Pause is misapplied and allowed to turn from consciousness and intentionality into procrastination or eternal postponement, the natural result is the hassle and expense of removing and disposing of branch after branch, the enormous trunk, and finally all those extensisve and developed roots.

As you develop the habit of effectively using Pause, be cautious and intentional, but do not allow yourself to merely defer the situation until later. If it needs to be dealt with, it should be handled well, which means it needs a Pause. But if it *does* need to be dealt with, the Pause shouldn't last very long.

Dealing with difficulties when they're small is one of the best ways to minimize them. In reality, this is the spirit of Pause. People who recognize this will see it in their results.

> *Dealing with difficulties when they're small is one of the best ways to minimize them.*

So don't be afraid of the hassle of dumping a pebble from your shoe or plucking a tiny shoot from the ground. You'll save yourself worlds of pain and trouble, and you'll probably make the situation easier for everyone around you as well.

In words attributed to Abraham Lincoln, "You cannot escape the responsibility of tomorrow by evading it today."[1] In fact, you often make it much harder and a lot worse by trying this. So Pause, but don't *wait*! When difficulties arise, Pause to consider and reflect so you can make the best choice, but deal with them quickly when action is needed.

Parts of Pause

In summary, there are several important parts of Pause. These include the following:

- When a difficult person presents a difficult situation, immediately respond by mentally removing yourself from the situation and relaxing for a few moments, stepping back from the emotion of the event and reflecting on what really matters in the interaction with the difficult person.

- Ask yourself if the difficulty is worth your time and attention in this instance or if it is just a possible distraction that has nothing to do with your real purpose. If the difficulty is meaningless, don't engage it. Move on.

- If you decide not to engage, make sure you aren't just putting off a conversation that will have to be dealt with later. Will it fester? If so, it's usually better to deal with it directly right away.

- If the difficulty is important enough to require your attention, ask yourself what tendencies you have (in general and today) for being difficult yourself. Control these tendencies so you stay in charge of your emotions, and don't let the difficult person take over for you.

- Once you and your difficult tendencies are under control, ask yourself what type of difficult person you are facing. Quickly identify who you are dealing with so you don't say all the wrong things or make mistakes because you misread the confrontation.

- Once you've decided that this is a difficulty worth dealing with, taken control of yourself so your emotions won't grab the reins, and identified generally what the difficult person is like, ask yourself what the best possible results of this interaction are. Then consider the most effective way to get those results.

- With all these tasks completed (whether this took three seconds or you arranged for a meeting in three days), you are now ready to move on to Step 2. Do not move on until you have used your Pause to mentally consider all these items. With practice, you can become very good at doing this quickly and thoroughly.

Pause is powerful, and it makes all the difference between success and failure in dealing with difficult people.

STEP 2

Empathy

*You never really understand a person until you
consider things from his point of view—...until you climb into
his skin and walk around in it.*

—ATTICUS IN HARPER LEE'S *TO KILL A MOCKINGBIRD*

CHAPTER 12

Empathy Matters

*The great gift of human beings is that we have the power of
empathy; we can all sense a mysterious connection to each other.*
— Meryl Streep

The second step in the Five-Step Peace Process of
dealing with difficult people and situations is to experience Empathy. Pause helps us slow down and assess the
situation, and Empathy helps us slow down and assess the
person.

The importance of Empathy in dealing with difficult
people is paramount. Those who hope to produce a positive outcome from a negative situation as often as possible
must learn to understand and appreciate the needs and
desires of the person causing the difficulty in order to
effectively meet them in the solution.

If a top leader approaches a difficult person and tries to
fix the problem without first trying to understand what is
making the person difficult or problematic, she probably
won't be called a top leader for long, as her leadership will

generally be ineffective. The first key to effectively solving a problem is to know what the real problem actually is.

> *The first key to effectively solving a problem is to know what the real problem actually is.*

This is why top leaders Pause, and it is also why they take time to Empathize before the Pause is over — long before they "handle" or "address" the problem. Sometimes the only thing the difficult person needs is the recognition and validation of his or her difficulties, efforts, or humanity. In such cases, failure to Empathize is obviously a failure to deal with the difficulty.

Other times, more than just Empathy is required. In such situations, while it is less obvious, a failure on the part of the leader to Empathize is almost always detrimental.

Recognize People as Such

In his book *The Magic of Thinking Big*, David J. Schwartz, Ph.D., teaches that a vital part of having confidence as a leader is learning to put people in proper perspective. When individuals don't have the proper perspective of people, they tend to either fear them too much or cause unnecessary levels of fear and intimidation around them. Both of these can get in the way of effective leadership.

The solution is largely based in Empathy, and when people learn to implement it, the results are powerful.

Schwartz explains that before you can put people in the right perspective, you need to get a balanced view of the other person. He says:

> Keep these two points in mind when dealing with people: first, the other fellow is important. Emphatically, he is important. Every human being is. But remember this, also: *You are important, too.* So when you meet another person, make it a policy to think, "We are just two important people sitting down to discuss something of mutual interest and benefit."[1]

As far as remembering your own importance in such situations, we already discussed a few key tactics for this in the chapters on Pause, and we will discuss the subject in further depth and detail in the chapters on Contribution. For now, let's address the power and significance of recognizing and remembering the other person's value.

The idea that the other person is important is in many ways the reason Empathy matters so much. It is precisely because top leaders know that others are important that they believe Empathy is vital, which in turn is why they are so effective at serving and leading people—even difficult ones.

Make it a policy to note the significance and value of the other person—even when he or she is difficult—from the start and throughout each interaction you have with people. This will make a huge difference in the way you approach every interaction. In fact, Empathy makes it more about your ongoing relationship than just the present interaction.

Part of Something Bigger

When a person Empathizes, she recognizes that each interaction, conversation, and situation involving herself and another human being is part of a bigger-picture relationship between two important people. This naturally changes the way she presents herself and the way she thinks about and ultimately treats every other person.

When an understanding of the importance of an individual encourages Empathy and right action, it likewise leads to powerful thinking and effective service and leadership.

If the other person's difficult nature or situation made him somehow cease to be important as a human being, Empathy would be less critical, though not less effective. But since even a difficult human being is an important one, top leaders know that Empathy is not only a powerful and extremely effective tool but also something they owe every individual due to their humanity. Recognizing the humanity in others and accounting for it in your approach to their difficulty is a vital aspect of servant leadership as well as personal and relationship success.

Those who hope to be effective at dealing with difficult people should understand that a good number of the biggest people problems are caused by a lack of Empathy. Empathy is essential to success, and feeling it also happens to be the *right* thing to do.

Pausing to recognize the importance of the other person naturally leads to Empathy, which is the only factor that can lead to a positive and right solution. If you haven't come to understand who the other person is, where he's coming from, what he wants and needs, what makes him tick, and especially that he really is important, you simply are not ready to deal with him. Period.

Successful people know that before they can hope to correctly deal with a situation, they have to understand what the situation is, why it's happening, and what could fix it. In dealing with difficult people, top leaders do not act first and ask questions later. They take the time to understand.

Paramount to Greatness

Movie critic Roger Ebert said, "I believe empathy is the most essential quality of civilization."[2] This is significant because he didn't say it was the most important quality *imaginable* but the most important *of civilization.* In other words, to have a powerfully bonded group of people effectively working together and dealing with each other to build something great, Empathy is paramount. And it takes leadership.

When it comes to dealing with people of any kind, difficult or otherwise, Empathy is crucial to both success and excellence. Those seeking greatness and excellence should remember that Empathy is both a helpful tool and an important character trait, which reflects on who they are as leaders and people.

This will make all the difference in your ability to correctly handle difficult people and situations, and the way you choose to use it is a reflection of who you are as a leader. In many ways, the ability to Empathize, and the dedication to doing so, is what separates the weak from the strong in servant leadership.

In short, Empathy matters! It will make a huge difference, both in your success and your wholeness as a leader. So plan on it. Learn to use it. Get good at it. And remember, the other person is important!

CHAPTER 13

Empathy Is *Not* Reflection or Projection

*Did you ever wonder if the person in the puddle
is real, and you're just a reflection of him?*
— FROM *CALVIN AND HOBBES* BY BILL WATTERSON

In understanding and pursuing the ability to Empathize with people, it is absolutely critical to recognize the difference between a reflection or a projection and an actual portrait or authentic understanding.

Top leaders know the importance of seeing the real person when Empathizing, not a reflection of who they are or a projection of who they think the other person probably is or ought to be. Reflecting and projecting are two of the most common mistakes when it comes to Empathizing, but it is possible to avoid them and extremely important to seek to do so.

City Walls

There is an old story of an elderly man sitting outside the wall of a medieval city. As the man sat beside the gate, a traveler approached and asked what type of people lived in the city.

The old man responded, "Well, what kind of people live in the town you come from?" He smiled as the traveler explained that, for the most part, they were good, honest, kindhearted, and generally well-to-do people. Then he replied, "I'd imagine you'll find about the same here."

The traveler continued into the city, and the old man went back to his people watching.

Later that day, another traveler came up to the old man and asked, "What kind of people live in this city?"

The old man responded with the same question as before and listened patiently as the traveler explained the mean-spirited, selfish, greedy cheats and thieves he'd known in his last city. When the traveler finished his rant, the old man nodded and solemnly pronounced, "I expect you'll find about the same here."

Of course the old man was referring to the same city in both instances, but as someone who had met and watched many people by the gate over the years, this man understood that we generally get what we expect from people and what we put forth ourselves.

This story is enlightening, as it points out one of the biggest traps of trying to choose Empathy. Sometimes before we get to the level of actually Empathizing with a person we're dealing with, we start trying to prejudge or assign motive to the person. We want to jump to the answers and solutions without spending the required time or effort on the important questions.

In such cases, rather than seeing people for who they truly are, we project our own misguided worldview onto them, assuming they'll behave in a way that supports our definition of how "that kind of person" will tend to act.

Although there *is* a place for proper judgment, and it's certainly not helpful to be so naïve as to believe no one will ever be difficult, it doesn't accomplish much to incorrectly label people as difficult in any particular way. In fact, doing so blinds us from seeing the real situation and makes it extremely difficult to live a genuinely happy or successful life.

This is clearly not the desired result, so those who seek to be leaders must learn to differentiate between assigning motive or *projecting* difficulties on others and actually seeing and Empathizing with the person they're dealing with.

Knowledge of the seven main types of difficult people can be helpful in this process if we take the time to really understand the difficult person. But if we jump to quick conclusions without really listening, we can make mistakes. And people mistakes are usually painful.

It is essential not to reflect or project but to try to understand. Stephen Covey said we should seek first to understand and then to be understood. He called this one of the seven habits of highly effective people.[1] This is excellent counsel.

Why is the person being difficult?

This is an extremely important question. Until you have an answer, it is hard — if not impossible — to move on to solutions.

Top leaders seek to understand. They ask themselves why the other person is being difficult, and they try to see things from the difficult person's viewpoint. This is Empathy.

CHAPTER 14

What *Is* Empathy?

[O]nly by cultivating empathy can we truly grow as people.
—JEN KNOX

Ben Harper said, "There's something in everyone only they know."[1] In reality, there are lots of these things that "only they know," and one of the main goals of Empathy is to try to discover what they are, specifically in relation to the difficulty at hand.

In almost every difficult situation or conflict, there is something—or possibly multiple factors—hidden in the heart of the difficult person that, if properly understood and addressed, would make the whole problem go away. This is a big assertion, and it is also true.

Are there exceptions? Yes, probably. But the statement is still largely accurate.

People generally aren't difficult without cause or reason, and seeking to learn the cause and reason in each situation is a vital step to finding the best solution. This is what Empathy is all about.

As we discussed earlier, recognizing that the other person is important and deserves to be Empathized with is the first rung on the ladder of Empathy. But what is the next? What is Empathy itself?

> *People generally aren't difficult without cause or reason, and seeking to learn the cause and reason in each situation is a vital step to finding the best solution.*

Most people have a basic understanding of what the word means. The world is full of phrases like "walk a mile in her shoes" and "look through his eyes," but it seems to be difficult for people to even remember to try let alone actually feel Empathy and feel it well.

Unfortunately, while almost everyone has a basic understanding of what Empathy is, almost no one knows how to actually bring it to a conscious level at will. This is challenging even to those who believe it is a valuable skill.

Yet top leaders have a different experience. They have taught themselves to stop and Empathize. It's almost like a second Pause. When confronted with a difficult person, top leaders Pause (going through all the parts of Step 1). Then they turn their attention to the other person and Pause again. They ask why the other person is being difficult. They don't want to move on until they have a satisfying answer to this crucial question.

Top leaders not only know what Empathy is and how much it matters. They also have an understanding of how to switch it on when confronted with a difficult person, and they are able to intentionally and effectively use the power of Empathy in their daily lives and relationships. Again, nearly all of them had to teach themselves to do this.

This is a huge part of what *makes* them top leaders, since dealing with people requires one to understand people and what motivates and drives them. That said, those who hope to become top leaders need to know how to Empathize so they can get good at it and make it a part of their normal routine, both in building relationships and teams and in dealing with the various difficult people who just happen to come along.

Actually, top leaders deal with more difficult people than others do. Why? Because they deal with more people in high-pressure and frequently changing situations. One way to tell how well you are doing in becoming a leader is to take note of how many difficult people cross your path.

And as you encounter more difficult people, it becomes increasingly important to teach yourself to do so effectively.

Ask the Right Questions

A big part of effective and authentic Empathy is learning to ask the right questions, both of yourself and of other people. Sometimes what is needed to Empathize is to directly ask questions of the person you're dealing with and then listen patiently and attentively to everything he or she says.

Other times, this might be the worst choice. Empathy may require you to ask yourself questions about the difficult person and answer them honestly while applying the Golden Rule (do unto others as you would have them do unto you) or the Platinum Rule (do unto others as they would have you do unto them).

In either case, asking the right questions of the right person at the right time is a great way to start the Empathy process, and it can lead to some powerful insights and understanding of people—which will bring incredible inspiration and creativity regarding what to do next.

Pause 1 (get rid of your inner difficult person and take charge with your inner best leader) is followed by Pause 2 (Empathize with the difficult person in front of you so you really understand him). These are the first two steps of the Peace Process: Pause and Empathize.

Ask the Person

When it comes to the questions a leader directly asks another person, they're generally personal and specific, based on who the leader is dealing with. The idea is to get the other person talking about herself in a way that reveals who she is, what she cares about, what motivates her, scares her, and drives her, what she wants, what holds her back, etc.

You don't need to ask all these questions. Just start getting to know the person.

On some occasions, leaders will come out and frankly or bluntly ask these things specifically. More often, they just ask the other person general questions about herself and let her share what she wants or thinks is important.

Throughout the conversation, the leader listens and seeks to understand the person and her needs and feelings. By listening and allowing her to talk about herself, in whatever way she wants, the leader allows her to paint a picture. This picture, then, enables the leader to figuratively "walk a mile in her shoes" or "take a peek through her eyes."

This is a powerful form of Empathy, although it is rarely available in the heat of a conflict with a difficult person. In fact, if you have the opportunity, this is most effectively accomplished long before any confrontation takes place.

Prospective leaders must learn to judge what method of Empathizing is needed in each situation, and sometimes they really should take time to sit down and ask the other person about who she is and what she wants.

Ask Yourself *as* the Other Person

Another way to achieve Empathy is to ask *yourself* in a rapid-fire succession the right questions about who and what the other person is, attempt to see through his eyes, and use what you learn to help enlighten and improve your response.

In using this approach, here are some of the most important questions top leaders ask themselves:

1. Is this person difficult or just having a difficult day?
2. Which of the seven main types of difficult people does this person most closely resemble?
3. Is this person difficult with everyone or just with me?
4. Why is this person being difficult right now?
5. Why has this person chosen to be difficult in general, with me and with other people?
6. What makes this person tick?
7. What does he or she want right now?
8. What are his or her goals, life purpose, and mission?
9. Is this current conflict about his or her life purpose or something else?
10. What is this *really* about?
11. What does he or she need?
12. How does he or she see the situation?

Asking these questions in your mind, even quickly during a conversation, can help increase your understanding of the situation and will drastically shift both the way you look at it and the way you respond to it.

Seek First to Understand and Then to Be Understood

The main point to remember in Empathy mode is that you really are seeking first to understand. This is what Empathy is all about. It is important because every person you'll ever deal with matters, regardless of how difficult he or she is.

As we get to the Agility and Contribution steps of the Peace Process, you'll come to more fully understand the role Empathy plays in the big picture. It is an absolutely vital step in the process.

> *Every person you'll ever deal with matters, regardless of how difficult he or she is.*

As you make it your habit to understand the people you're dealing with, instead of focusing purely on how they are difficult, you'll find yourself loving them more and better, which will allow you to better serve and lead them.

As Robert Kegan of Harvard said, "When we take the risk of really witnessing another human being, when we validate their human experience, we risk becoming recruited to their welfare."[1] This sounds like a danger to effective leadership, but when it is given its proper place among the other parts of the process, it can only be a positive and powerful asset.

When you are "recruited to their welfare" and they know it, they will be able to trust you and your leadership on a whole new level. Some difficult people may choose not to trust you, but most will.

Even when what you choose as the best response isn't exactly what they wanted, the people around you will come to trust that you've got their backs, and they'll support you more fully for your Empathy.

Pay the Price to Care

When you pay the price to understand and care about the people you interact with, your relationships can't help but benefit and grow. Not only will Empathy make you better at dealing with individual cases of difficult people; it will also make you a better leader as you are able to serve the people around you in the very best ways. As you become recruited to their welfare and they see you fighting for their interests, you'll build a team of people who are ready to sacrifice for the bigger picture and higher purpose because they don't feel like they have to spend all their time proving they're important. They know they matter, and they know you know that too.

As a popular saying that is embraced by top leaders such as John C. Maxwell puts it, "People don't care how much you know until they know how much you care."[2] As your people feel how much you care about them and everyone else, they'll be ready to listen to what you know, fight for what you envision, and follow where you lead. And in the process, you'll be able to deal with the difficult ones much better.

CHAPTER 15

Thoughts on Pause and Empathy: Use Discernment

Consider the source....Don't be a fool by listening to a fool.
—Sylvester Stallone

Throughout the process of learning to deal with difficult people—especially when it comes to striking down your own inner difficult person—it is extremely important to always remember that nobody is undifficult all the time.

We're all difficult at times in our lives, and sometimes we're more sensitive and susceptible to difficulty around us. No matter how great any of us are, we still have times when we are a little more difficult than usual and other times when we are a *lot* harder to take. And on top of that, we have times when we are more likely to react harshly or intensely to difficult people around us.

In short, we all have our moments. Learning to recognize the difference between a difficult person and a person having a difficult moment is an important part of Empathy and a significant part of learning to effectively deal with difficult people.

> *Learning to recognize the difference between a difficult person and a person having a difficult moment is an important part of Empathy.*

Difficult ≠ Difficult

Sometimes the best way to deal with "difficult people" is to simply forgive their momentary lapse of self-control, excuse their unusual display of less-than-cordial behavior, and remember who they usually are.

When you know how to differentiate between a really difficult individual and a person in a really difficult mood, it's a lot easier to correctly handle each situation. Sometimes, with a person in a difficult moment or mood, the best course of action is to "give the guy a break."

Now, we're not saying this is always the best approach, and you certainly shouldn't use this principle as an excuse to duck out of important conversations when they are needed. But there is a time and a place where your *best* move is simply to ignore a difficult behavior. As author Mark Frost wrote in *The Grand Slam*, "sometimes the greatest advice is best expressed in silence."[1]

Other times, what is needed is a swift and firm response to what looks to an outsider like "the same behavior." Still other times, the best option is actually approaching the individual and offering help and support.

It all depends on the situation. This is what Agility is all about — as we'll discuss in the next chapter. But it's worth seeing how the first three steps fit together before we move on specifically to Agility.

As you learn and apply the principles of Pause and Empathy, you'll start to recognize more options and which ones are likely better than others. Within Pause, Empathy, and Agility, top leaders use discernment.

And when it comes to dealing with difficult people, Empathy, Agility, and discernment matter a great deal. The rule here is not complex or even difficult to apply when we make a point of actually remembering it in the moment. All you really have to do is think before you act.

Before you decide how to deal with anyone about anything, make sure you understand the situation you're dealing with and who the person is. Then act accordingly.

Problem → Solution

Specifically, once leaders have effectively Paused and Empathized, it's time to be Agile. They start to see the various options in front of them, and they get excited to consider the ideas gained during Pause and Empathy that will determine which choice is best.

The principle of using discernment doesn't change anything in the pattern most people follow in dealing with situations. It just asks us to give necessary weight to each step, especially the first three, *before* we pick our overall response to the stimulus caused by a difficult person.

In short, when top leaders assess a situation and choose a solution, they don't just look at the picture in front of them and make a snap decision on how to react. They Pause, Empathize, and think about possible options.

Clearly Pause and Empathy will leave us better prepared to come up with the right solution than merely judging the behavior itself and assuming everyone is exactly the same and does things for the same reasons. The right kind of Agility, therefore, depends heavily on the right kind of Pause and Empathy.

For example, let's say your assistant Susan has cultivated and developed a reputation as someone who's always on time, always kind and respectful to everyone, and always where she needs to be. But then one day, she shows up to work a few minutes late, seems flustered and absentminded all day, and even snaps at you and other people. You should probably approach the situation differently than you would the same behavior from Katy, who is consistently late, easily irritated, constantly stirring up office controversy, and always hard to find when you need her.

The solutions to these problems are different because the problems themselves are different. Not all difficult people are difficult for the same reasons.

If a difficult behavior is unusual in the person you're dealing with, that should count for something in your assessment of the problem, and it should affect the way you choose to handle it. Using discernment means you take time to carefully evaluate the trouble in front of you, and then you determine your response based on the findings, all before you move into the action phase.

Pay Attention

As you apply the principles and techniques you learn in this book, make sure you use proper discernment in dealing with people.

Pay the price to understand the problem before you rush in with a million "solutions."

> *The best answer for Susan isn't the best one for Katy, and the best answer on Friday isn't always the best one on Tuesday.*

The best answer for Susan isn't the best one for Katy, and the best answer on Friday isn't always the best one on Tuesday. Consider all the factors in each situation, not just a couple of them, before you decide how to fix things.

In short, the Five-Step Peace Process includes always using discernment in dealing with difficult people.

STEP 3

Agility

Becoming limitless involves mental agility; the ability to quickly grasp and incorporate new ideas and concepts with confidence.

— LORII MYERS

CHAPTER 16

Innovative Agility

A wonderful gift may not be wrapped as you expect.
— Jonathan Lockwood Huie

The third step in the Five-Step Peace Process is Agility. This is a crucially important step, one that distinctly separates creative thinkers, innovators, and leaders from their less-successful counterparts.

The ability to face a situation and respond with Agility, rather than with rigidness or narrow-mindedness, is a vital leadership trait and often means the difference between a poor to mediocre solution and one that combines qualities like ingenuity, creativity, inspiration, innovation, and lasting impact.

The Agility step comes after an inwardly directed Pause and a period of Empathy and, combined with the later Contribution phase, is the perfect transition between reflection and effective action.

Up until now, in Pause and Empathy, the leader has been focused completely on assessing the situation and the difficult person — on evaluating the factors that make up the difficulty and the obstacles that stand between himself and a solution—but he has not yet begun considering the possible courses of action or the best solutions.

Agility is the phase in which he makes this transition. Now, rather than merely seeing past events and factors, he starts to consider present possibilities and future impact.

He asks himself, "How *could* I respond to this, and how would each possible option change things for the future of everyone involved?"

Yet the word *agility* itself implies more than just finding and implementing solutions. It suggests a special method of doing so in which prospective leaders open their eyes in a whole new way, allowing themselves to see every available option, no matter how unconventional, and assess each for its merits.

This is the time to be innovative and generate creative and original ideas. This type of Agile vision is powerful and even beautiful because it produces results that sometimes seem beyond normal human capacity. By opening themselves up to the possibilities and seeking options and sources from everywhere, true leaders are able to feel inspiration and then inspire and help others—even difficult people—behave and respond in incredible ways, as their very best selves.

By not limiting themselves to normally prescribed or traditionally used solutions and responses, top leaders are able to see boundless potential opportunity in each situation and find the absolute *best* solution, rather than being controlled by any past failings of others to do so. And if it is best, they have the option of choosing the traditional path as well.

This is Agility.

Freedom, Agility, and Opportunity

William Barrett said, "Our freedom is the way in which we are able to let the world open before us."[1] This is something that successful people understand. In order to be truly free and able in the world, you have to get your vision and thinking to a level where you actually see all the freedom and opportunity in the world.

Top leaders have learned that it doesn't matter how much opportunity exists in the world if a person can't see it or isn't even looking for it. If you aren't actively seeking opportunities, you'll likely find significantly fewer of them than someone who is.

This is a simple truth, yet putting it into action separates highly successful people from those who are unsuccessful. Successful people look for and recognize opportunity, while unsuccessful people wait for it to come around and sometimes don't even recognize it or take action when it does. Then they write themselves off as unlucky.

This same principle is at work when it comes to dealing with difficult people. We merely need to substitute the word *option* for *opportunity*, and it becomes clear that when one actively seeks creative and ingenious options in difficult situations, he'll find them more often and be able to work out the best solutions for successfully handling the difficulties.

Conversely, when he sits around waiting for the best option to present itself at his feet, he'll be considerably less likely to handle the situation as well, and he'll frequently end up blaming the mediocrity of his choice on the lack of good options.

Agility means actively seeking to see *all* the options, so the final decision won't be limited by a lack of freedom in choosing. Options are really just opportunities, and leaders look for opportunities!

Painting the Rainbow

The idea in all this is to paint a rainbow of opportunity in each difficult situation and with each difficult person before deciding which color to paint the brick road leading out of it. And by the way, this is not a traditional rainbow, limited to the same old seven colors we learned in elementary school. This rainbow may include red, orange, yellow, green, blue, indigo, and violet, but who says it shouldn't incorporate plain old purple as well as mauve, burgundy, aubergine, xanadu, mikado, sarcoline, and everything in between!

The more colors you can think of and add to the rainbow of choice, the more likely you'll be to come up with one that really works. It might even be amazing because of its creativity, apparent randomness, and *brilliance* at dealing with the situation in a way that's better than anyone thought possible.

When the possibilities are endless and you take the time to sort through them to choose the best, the chances of that "best" being top-notch are much higher than if you pick only from the traditional seven colors of the rainbow.

Practice and Rescript

Painting the rainbow is what Agility is all about, and doing so gives you the opportunity to exponentially increase your chances of success. It dramatically improves your ability to come up with the *right* solution in every situation. So start painting rainbows, and don't be afraid to mix in all sorts of new or obscure colors!

As you do this, you'll find your thinking and vision expanding in immeasurable ways, allowing you to improve your life, projects, and relationships. When confronted with a difficult person, quickly Pause and get grounded, Empathize so you're considering viable solutions, and then think of all the promising ways you could deal with the situation—and the consequences of each option.

This puts power into your next choice. And in reality, it can happen in just a few seconds. This is especially true if you practice. This may be the most important exercise in the book, or anywhere, to increase your skills at dealing with difficult people.

Specifically, think of past dealings with difficult people, and rescript what happened—this time using Pause, Empathy, and Agility. Most people loop hard conversations and interactions with difficult people over and over in their minds, but they tend to focus on the negative. This only makes the past difficulty even more frustrating in the present.

Try flipping the whole scenario. Replay past encounters with difficult people, but this time rescript the entire event. Picture yourself acting differently, using Pause, Empathy, and Agility. Practice this until you are really good at this and respond with such amazing words or actions that it defuses the difficulty.

For each difficult encounter you can remember, practice by coming up with at least three highly successful solutions that defuse the difficulty. This will make you better in future interactions. Practice is powerful.

Seriously, take a few moments and practice this right now.

Turn this kind of practice into a habit. If you do this well, you will become increasingly skilled at dealing with difficult people.

> *Difficult people will mostly remain difficult, whatever you do. The purpose of the process isn't to change them; it's to change you.*

Using the Five-Step Peace Process doesn't mean you'll easily turn every interaction with a difficult person to flowers and perfume in two seconds flat. Difficult people are…well, difficult. And they'll mostly remain difficult, whatever you do. The purpose of the process isn't to change them; it's to change you.

You have the real power, after all. No matter how difficult a person is, if you apply the Five-Step Peace Process, something extremely important will happen. The person may still be very difficult, but one factor will be different: You will be at your best. You will be your most grounded, inspired, wise, innovative, and caring self.

This will make a significant difference. You'll get the best result possible, even if the other person remains difficult. Why? Because you will be your best, not your mediocre or weakest self.

So practice. Replay past difficult encounters in your mind, and rescript each of them with your best self, using Pause, Empathy, and Agility.

These work. Moreover, they are genuinely powerful. By practicing them, you'll prepare yourself to easily respond at your best when the real thing comes again.

Of course, "Out with the rigid and in with the Agile" tends to mean "out with the limits of old thinking and in with the possibilities of future growth and progress!" This is what people who want to be top leaders should be trying to accomplish, and Agility is what will get them there.

CHAPTER 17

Don't Jump
the Gun

Forgiveness is the attribute of the strong.
—MAHATMA GANDHI

Agility is powerful! When leaders understand that they
get to pick their response from any number of options,
great things can happen. When they use creativity and
innovation to come up with excellent solutions, they
become skilled at turning difficulty into opportunity.

So when considering options, leaders should remember
that even in an effort to address problems while they're
small, it's crucial to avoid creating unnecessary problems
out of issues that were too insignificant to matter or should
have simply been forgiven or overlooked instead.

As we said above, it's important not to let small wounds
fester into huge ones and not to make a big deal out of
every little thing. With a truly Agile mindset, top leaders
realize that they get to choose how they react! Sure, there

was a difficulty, but does that mean you have to make a big deal out of it? Depending on the situation, Agility says no.

After the Honeymoon

Sarah was a happy bride. She had gone through a quick courtship. But she was fully dedicated to her husband, and all evidence pointed toward him being none other than an angel from heaven.

Imagine her surprise when, a few short weeks after the honeymoon, she found that her brand-new husband was constantly doing little things that bugged and irritated her. She had heard of this happening with other people, but somehow she thought she would be the exception. The annoyances weren't huge, but when added together, they certainly could have fallen under the label of "difficult" without raising any alarm.

After a few weeks of this consistent behavior from the man she'd assumed was perfect, she decided something had to be done. She just couldn't take it anymore!

Sarah's mother had always told her to reflect before acting, especially in relationships that really mattered. One frequently repeated statement particularly stood out in her memory: "Sometimes it's better to be happy than to be right."

So she decided to take her notebook with her on a lunch break. As she sat on the bench outside the library where she worked, she started to list what was bothering her. After a few minutes of this, she figured her list was long enough to tackle, so she read over it again, asking herself,

"Is this something to address and change or something to accept and forgive?"

As she went down the list, item by item, she found there were a few issues she really needed to talk through with the love of her life but several others she needed to just let go. Not everything annoying was truly unbearable.

When she had finished, she went through again and made two separate lists—one with items she and her spouse needed to discuss and consider together and one with issues she just needed to let go and never worry about again.

She put the list to talk through with her husband back in her notebook and determined to address the items as soon as possible, so she wouldn't be getting mad at him for things he didn't even know about. She read through the other list a few times, resolved to excuse the items on it, and crumpled it up for the garbage, never to be worried about again.

Back at home after work, she put the list to address in a drawer for a month. When the month was over, she pulled it out and repeated the item-by-item analysis. At the end, she found there was only one issue she really felt strongly about. The rest she forgave and even embraced.

As for the one item left, she brainstormed many ways to deal with it. She got creative, considered various options, and pondered the best approach. One of the ideas from her brainstorming just kept nagging at her brain, so eventually she decided to listen. "I just need to pray about this," she told herself. "I'll ask God to help my husband fix this or help me accept it or both—whatever He thinks is best."

This was a surprising conclusion for Sarah. Many of the people she knew constantly pointed out flaws in their spouses and talked about trying to change them. But she didn't like the way most of their relationships struggled, so she brainstormed alternative solutions.

She began praying fervently, day after day, for a miracle—for God to either help her husband change or help her change so she would be able to accept his differences. After just four days, her husband surprised her by suddenly bringing up the topic at dinner.

"I've been trying to work on a bad habit," he told her. "I'm wondering if you would be willing to help me."

"Sure," she said. "What is it?"

Then he started talking about the very item from her list. At first, she wondered if he had found the paper and read it. But it became clear that he had felt the need to improve in this area on his own. Together, with his lead, they came up with ideas for change and made a plan.

He changed much more effectively and quickly than if she had whined at him about her frustrations because now it was his idea, and he was seriously invested in making the change.

Forgiveness *Is* Allowed

This is an important point. You should strive to deal with problems while they're small, but that doesn't mean you have to make a problem out of everything that's small and potentially negative. We can't stress enough how much Agility of mind matters to leadership excellence.

The Agile-minded leader knows that it is absolutely okay, even great, to forgive little things and move on. Minor difficulties in people's character can be ignored and accepted, and sometimes that's the best way to handle them.

If there is another effective way to deal with a difficult person or a person in difficulty, using Agility to think of and ponder solutions will bring up various inventive and often unexpected ideas and plans. This nearly always increases a leader's effectiveness.

Don't be afraid to excuse people when it's right. The important thing is to make sure the problem isn't one that will naturally get bigger if you don't do something about it now. If there will be repercussions from disregarding it, don't. Also, if you're not prepared to truly forgive and forget, it may be something that should be addressed.

But first, use Agility. Consider your options. Brainstorm creative solutions. Ponder possible plans.

When it's something that can't really be let go, leaders aren't afraid to get into it. But they are also willing and ready to pardon or overlook matters that don't have weight in the long run—or else to find effective alternative solutions.

Make It Happen and Move On

One of the benefits of Agility in leadership—and in all relationships and interactions with difficult people—is the realization that there are all sorts of options, and not every difficultly that comes up has to be a "thing."

As those who seek to become excellent at dealing with difficult people make a point of addressing problems while they're still small, letting go of what is too insignificant to worry about, and genuinely forgiving what they should, they often find this diminishes the difficult situations they get into and the number of difficult people they have to deal with. By getting good at all these options, leaders are better prepared to face the really difficult people and situations that *do* come.

The combination of these principles is incredibly powerful and extremely important. Successful and happy people forgive what they can and address the situations they need to, creatively and wisely. They do all this as soon as possible and move on. It's very simple and also has the charming effect of making life much simpler. Agility expands their options and effectiveness.

CHAPTER 18

Don't Escalate

Between an uncontrolled escalation and passivity, there is
a demanding road of responsibility that we must follow.
— Dominique de Villepin

The main idea in this chapter is similar to the last point, but some important nuances particularly need to be addressed in preparation for facing difficult people.

Don't Overreact

The first step of not escalating is simply to not overreact at the beginning of an issue or at any stage along the way. Make a point of recognizing and understanding the real problem, and don't respond to a pillow fight with a nuclear bomb.

This is a fairly simple concept, yet one of the most common traits among difficult people is to employ this tactic of overreacting. So whether you're dealing with an overreactor or any other type of difficult person, make sure you don't overreact yourself. Recognize a pillow fight as such, and respond accordingly. Agile leaders realize that doing this is an excellent way to avoid unnecessary conflicts as well as overescalation of the necessary ones.

Don't Be Mr. One-Up

Agility-minded leaders focus on being the bigger person, and often the best way to do this is to remember not to make a point of *saying* you're the bigger person, either literally or figuratively.

When dealing with a situation or difficulty turns into a game of one-upmanship, you've missed the mark. You're turning it into an escalating battle of who's coolest, best, or even right instead of actually trying to get the problem handled. While this is an option revealed by Agility, top leaders know that it isn't a very good one in most cases, so they avoid it.

Agility does not mean being willing to accept really bad options above good ones. One-upmanship is a type of escalation that not only makes the conflict bigger than it should be but also distracts from the point of the conflict itself.

In fact, the Escalator or Overreactor could easily be an eighth type of difficult person. Don't fall into this trap.

When a leader trying to deal with a difficult person effectively gives in to his inner Mr. One-Up, he usually ends up having a huge battle in which the original problem often becomes almost impossible to solve. Top leaders talk about the real issue(s) and choose to actually be the bigger person rather than trying to logically or emotionally prove they are.

Don't Start What You Can't Finish

When it comes to escalation, Agility provides a reminder that whatever level you take a conflict to is what the difficult person is going to have on his or her mind the next time there's an issue. So if you don't want a difficult person to escalate the situation when he or she has a problem with you in the future, do your best to avoid doing so now.

In fact, as a general guideline, try to come to a solution at the lowest possible level of aggression and difficulty achievable while still effectively dealing with the problem itself. Your goal usually should not be to really "give them a piece of your mind" or "show them who's boss."

> *As a general guideline, try to come to a solution at the lowest possible level of aggression and difficulty achievable while still effectively dealing with the problem itself.*

If you make it about the power struggle instead of the point you really care about, you'll probably lose your real point, and the power struggle will be all that's left. You have the power in this, no matter how difficult the other person is.

When the power struggle is all that's left, you really have nothing to win unless what you truly wanted was to show the person you're tougher than he or she is. And if that's the case, we'll refer you back to the first principle of dealing with difficult people: Don't be a difficult person yourself.

Don't Be a Jerk

Of course, you already know this by now, but we're here to warn you that it will be extremely tempting in emotional situations for you to revert to your inner Ms. Difficult! When embracing Agility and considering all the options, more than a few bad ones will pop up in your mind, and giving in to one of them can seem very appealing. The point is to be on guard and not let it happen.

When you're in the moment, dealing with someone who's inordinately difficult, it may be hard for you to stay relaxed and in control and to deal with him in the right way, no matter how many great principles you know. That's why Pause, Empathy, and Agility are so vital.

So be prepared for your emotions to try to get you riled, and instead keep your cool. Don't make it personal. Don't make it about you. But do make it as small as it can reasonably and effectively be. Deescalate whenever possible.

In short, the idea in all this is to stay relaxed. Be at your best. Remember what the real issue is, don't be distracted from it by any of the difficulty around you, and don't let the difficult person call the shots.

As you stay in control of yourself (it's easy with Pause, Empathy, and Agility, but very, very hard without them), your control of the situation and the outcome will be considerably greater than if you allow yourself to be baited or sidetracked. Keep control, and keep the matter small. Don't let the difficulty get bigger than it needs to be by adding extra problems to the one you're trying to solve.

This is one of the best tools for dealing with difficult people using Agility, and it will also make you a great example to those who look to you for guidance on how to approach similar people and situations. Use Agility to find a creative solution that solves the problem without escalating it.

Prospective leaders who master this Five-Step Peace Process will set the stage for excellence in the way they and all their associates deal with difficult people and conflict in general.

CHAPTER 19

Be Adaptable, Ego-Free, and Ready for Change!

A mind is like a parachute. It does not work if it is not open.
— FRANK ZAPPA

A huge part of Agility is having an open mind — one that is willing to be changed and influenced. This is key to an adaptable approach in life.

The people who are most successful at dealing with difficult people are those who genuinely listen to the other person, look at what the problem is, see all the possibilities, and aren't afraid to give up old ideas or policies when the solution calls for them to change themselves.

Einstein said, "The measure of intelligence is the ability to change."[1] Oftentimes, the factor to be altered is something as small as the way the leader sees the individuals or situations involved. The adjustment is especially easy in such cases because all that needs to change is the leader's own mind.

While that doesn't necessarily sound easy for everyone, effective leaders who develop the qualities of Agility and adaptability will be ready to do it at the drop of a hat, knowing how much impact it can have when done well.

This is essential to servant leadership because the ability to change effectively and quickly when needed is especially important for resolving conflict and dealing with difficult people. Naturally, as the principle of Agility clearly implies, for leaders dealing with difficult people, the answer is not always to modify who they are or what they're doing. But when it is, they should be humble, adaptable, and Agile enough to recognize the need and act quickly to make the situation better.

Even the Leader...

The most crucial point in all this is that in order to be Agile, leaders must be adaptable and also realize that they themselves are not infallible. It is important for them to remember who they are and what they stand for when they're dealing with difficult people. (And they certainly shouldn't be compromising important aspects of their mission or purpose just to pacify annoying or problem-creating people.) But also, there is absolutely a time to listen to the concerns of others and learn from what they have to say.

Even top leaders aren't always right or perfect in their approach, vision, thinking, or actions. In fact, even the best of leaders can and will make mistakes and fall prey to personal weaknesses or blind spots.

This is pretty much true of everyone, but leaders *know* they won't always get it right. And in the spirit of Agility, they listen to their people and mentors and watch for signs and cues that they need to change something in themselves or their ideas. This matters, and everyone who wants to be a great leader should remember to use Agility.

George Bernard Shaw is often credited with saying, "[T]hose who cannot change their minds cannot change anything."[2] People who want to make big and powerful changes in the world and in the lives of others absolutely must become adaptable. They have to learn to recognize their own fallibility and change themselves when needed.

If Agility means including and considering all the colors as part of the rainbow, it naturally includes the possibility that the difficult person is bringing forward a legitimate concern about the leader or

> *"[T]hose who cannot change their minds cannot change anything."*
> *— often attributed to George Bernard Shaw*

the situation—one that ought to be taken with gratitude and interest and applied to the future of how the leader behaves and approaches life, even if the person bringing it up didn't put it in the most tactful or respectful terms.

When it comes to Agility, leaders understand that the answer isn't always about how the difficult person can change. When you're the one who needs to change, the best thing to do is get excited that someone helped you see where you were wrong so you can adapt accordingly and be a better and more effective person!

A Cheer for Your Success

As Marcus Aurelius put it, "If someone can prove me wrong and show me my mistake in any thought or action, I shall gladly change. I seek the truth, which never harmed anyone: the harm is to persist in one's own self-deception and ignorance."[3]

We're not saying that leaders ought to bow to everything any difficult person has to say and instantly convert to his or her way of seeing things; this would clearly be the wrong approach. But during the moments that call for Agility, leaders listen and look deep enough to see when there is merit in the proposals or suggestions of the person they're dealing with, and they don't let their ego get in the way of the right solution, even when it is presented by a difficult person.

Make the Change and Move to What's Next

This is one of the most important aspects of Agility, and in fact, of dealing with difficult people. In order to be effective, leaders should listen and change when they're wrong and apologize when and where they can. They should also take a stand when it is needed, doing so wisely and productively. Agility is about considering all the options and choosing the best one in any given situation.

Being sincere and humble and recognizing and taking responsibility when you are wrong can go a long way!

Such an attitude also allows for a firmer and better-received reprimand or stance when you aren't the one who needs a change.

Those who get really good at this will be much more effective at pretty much everything, since what it means is faster, better, and more permanent change to themselves and quick solutions to problems when changes are needed elsewhere.

This approach to life will make people who adopt it happier, stronger, and more successful—and improve their impact on the difficult people who come around. Again, some people will stay difficult no matter what a leader does, but at least the leader who applies Pause, Empathy, and Agility will be at his or her very best in the situation—regardless of what the difficult person chooses.

CHAPTER 20

Agility: The Conquering Hero

If you are losing faith in human nature,
go and watch a marathon.
— KATHRINE SWITZER AND ROGER ROBINSON

Let's consider some examples of how Agility works. Remember the story of Jacob and Sacia, whom we met in chapter one? Sacia frequently played the Diva, and Jacob was trying to hire someone to fill his own job after he received a promotion.

When we left Jacob, he was starting to think that the only course of action was to fire Sacia. After reading about her Diva behavior, maybe you also thought that firing her was really the only good choice.

Always Pause

But before we take action with Jacob and let her go, let's execute the first three steps of the Peace Process. First, let's Pause. Take a deep breath. Relax. Smile.

This is easier for us as readers to do in the case of Sacia because she isn't in front of us, being difficult and bringing up frustrating emotions. But it's helpful to practice anyway. So Pause. Smile again. Put yourself in your own optimum mindset. Think of yourself right now as your very best leader self.

If it helps, picture someone you have met who acts like a Diva quite often. Now use Pause to relax and get in a state of being where you are in charge of your own emotions and feelings.

Be Empathetic

Next, use Empathy. Why might Sacia be acting like a Diva? Is she insecure? Is she afraid? Of what? Is she intimidated by you? Is she a frustrated perfectionist who is always unhappy with herself?

Use your imagination: Why is Sacia being a Diva? This might be more effective if you think of a real person in your own life. Why is that person a Diva? Insecurity? Fear? Intimidation? Frustrated perfectionism? Something else? What?

Now take the next step. How will she feel if she gets fired? How will the people around her feel if she gets promoted? Empathy includes thinking through the whole situation and how your choices will affect everyone involved. Moreover, how will *you* feel if she's fired? How will *you* feel if she stays?

If you know a Diva and can think through these feelings, great. If not, how do you think Jacob and Sacia will feel after she is either fired or promoted? As you consider this, you are engaging Empathy. Of course, it's more realistic if you are applying these theoretical questions to an actual Diva in your life.

Get Agile

Now that you have Paused, relaxed, and used Empathy to think about the needs of Jacob, Sacia, or a real-life Diva from your own experiences, go to Agility. What are the possible outcomes? What can Jacob do?

He could fire Sacia, yes. He could also promote her. The truth is, if you're like most people, neither of these actions feels complete. Both leave you feeling a bit frustrated. So be creative. Use Agility. What are some other options?

Maybe there is a different job where Sacia won't be leading people but can focus on projects and not get so caught up in her difficult tendencies. Maybe Jacob knows a client or friend who would benefit from Sacia's strengths in a different role where her weaknesses wouldn't be so problematic.

How does that option feel? Keep brainstorming. Are there other good alternatives? Maybe Jacob could have a heartfelt discussion with Sacia and put her on probation, a time to work on overcoming her bad habits. Or maybe, more positively, he could give her a chance to prove herself before the next promotion and ask her to outline a plan to fix her Diva behavior.

If you start to feel like you've found a decent solution, brainstorm even more. You might be on the verge of a truly great idea or two. For example, maybe Jacob could leave Sacia in her current job—not promote her or fire her. And he could start mentoring her to be more effective. He might have her read this book to learn about the seven major types of difficult people and then discuss with her how *she personally* would work with a difficult Diva in her own department under her leadership. Jacob might learn a lot from Sacia (and about Sacia) by doing this.

Of course, none of these options should be pursued just to avoid being a leader and doing the hard thing. If firing Sacia is the right action, so be it. But top leaders learn to first use Pause and Agility to consider how to effectively help Divas overcome their weaknesses and emphasize their strengths. Likewise, Jacob should only undertake the project if Sacia really can overcome her behaviors. But at least now Jacob has options.

Agility is incredibly powerful. Without it, we just aren't at our best as leaders. With it, it's amazing what ideas can come.

What other options can you come up with for Jacob to help him successfully deal with Sacia—preferably with a true win–win solution? Use your Agility and brainstorm. Practice this with fictional Sacia in mind, and you'll be better at it when a real-life Diva or other difficult person comes along.

Other Examples

Let's practice this process again. Remember Karen and her coworker Jeremy from chapter two? Jeremy was annoyingly bossy, always telling Karen what to do, including almost forcing her to immediately buy life insurance—even though it was really none of his business.

If you've ever dealt with a Boss in your life, you know how difficult this can be. What would you do if you were Karen, now that you know the first three steps of the Peace Process?

Of course, you'd Pause. You'd take enough time to Pause effectively and get emotionally strong. Next, you would use Empathy to try to understand Jeremy and why he behaves as he does. Once you were fully in charge of your emotions and had a sense of concern for Jeremy as a good person who is just making bad choices, you'd brainstorm solutions. You'd engage Agility.

What can Karen do? Take a few moments to come up with some ideas. This is valuable practice. Most people struggle with this at first. This is natural. But it's important to get good at it. So think about any Boss in your real life. Use Pause to get relaxed and in a state of mind that brings out your best. Then use Empathy to consider why this person might act this way.

Once you have done both of these first two steps, go to Agility. What are the possibilities in dealing with the Boss in your life? If you find this too hard, do it for fictional Karen. How can she effectively deal with Jeremy?

There are no wrong answers here—just ideas and options. But that's the point! You want to brainstorm as many as possible. You want to get good at thinking up a lot of possibilities. You're practicing Agility, so the more options you can come up with, the better.

Seriously, how could you help Karen deal with Jeremy?

Another Round

How did that go? If it was easy, that's excellent. If it was hard, that's great too. You are practicing a new skill, one that is worth learning. You will use it every day if you become good at it, and it will have an enormous influence on your effectiveness and success in life.

So keep trying, even if it feels difficult at first. Like learning to cook or to shoot free throws for your basketball team, you might not be fantastic at first. But practice can quickly increase your skills.

Let's try another one. Remember Carol and Mike from chapter six? Mike is Carol's partner. He frequently volunteers for projects and enthusiastically promises big results. But then he fails to show up or follow through. He's the Bungee Jumper, always positive and upbeat but never there when it's time to take action. Even if he does show up, he waits until it's too late to ask for help. So things fall through the cracks and nobody can really depend on him.

If you were Carol, what would you do? Practice using Pause.

Then take a few minutes and Empathize. Why would the Bungee Jumper be this way? What is making him choose this behavior? What are his weaknesses and, more important, what are his strengths?

Next, use Agility. What are the possible ways Carol can respond to Mike that will make a difference? Just talking to him obviously doesn't work, so what other options does she have?

Brainstorm as many options as you can think of. Take the time right now to practice this. Again, if you were learning to cook, you'd practice preparing a dish several times at least, or if you were practicing free throws, you'd stay on the court shooting for at least twenty or thirty minutes — maybe a lot more. Do the same with this exercise. Practice using Agility to come up with possible solutions.

Practice Makes Perfect

One of the benefits of reading a book about difficult people is that you don't have to suffer the emotional frustration or relationship problems that come with practicing this vital leadership skill on real people. Yes, you will want to use this process with real people, but hopefully you'll be a little better at this by the time you need it in real life — because you will have practiced it a few times beforehand.

If you've done the exercises above in this chapter, wonderful. If not, don't cheat yourself by skipping them. Dealing with difficult people is an essential skill for any leader and, for that matter, every person. So practice it here as you read. It will take only a few minutes, but it will have a significant impact on your mind and habits when you face a difficult person in real life.

Once you have practiced and visualized using Pause, Empathy, and Agility with Sacia, Jeremy, and Mike, don't stop there. Go back to the short stories at the beginning of chapters three, four, five, and seven. Reread the brief accounts of difficult people like Melanie (the Bureaucrat), Lance (the Victim), Teresa (the Autocrat), and Miranda (the Politician), and practice using Pause, Empathy, and Agility with each of them.

Just going through the Peace Process these seven times, once with each of the major types of difficult people, will make you much more effective at dealing with difficult people. Don't skip this. Don't cheat yourself. Enjoy this incredibly valuable leadership practice right now, right here.

Doing so will make a lasting difference in your ability to effectively deal with difficult people. As we said at the beginning of this book, you're going to encounter difficult people. Plan on. Prepare for it. Become good at it. This is essential leadership training.

Again, reread the stories at the beginnings of chapters one through seven (hopefully you have already done some of them!) and practice using Pause, Empathy, and Agility for each. The main goal is to train your mind to be Agile and creative in brainstorming multiple ways to deal with any difficult person or situation. After you have completed this practice, return to this point in the book and keep reading.

Going Agile

The possibilities and potential solutions discussed here are only a small fraction of the ones available to a creative and Agile leader, but we hope they've given you a taste of some of the less-frequently considered options and answers that ought to be a part of anyone's repertoire when it comes to dealing with difficult people.

Remember that as a leader or prospective leader, you are in control of yourself. You get to decide how to respond to difficult people, and that doesn't always mean a fight or "putting them in their place." Agility allows leaders the freedom to be imaginative and innovative in the solutions they explore and apply.

Your ability to best deal with these situations is limited mostly by your skill in Pausing and seeing the possibilities around you, so get creative. Think differently. Look for new, unexpected solutions. Francis Bacon wisely counseled, "[T]hey are ill discoverers that think there is no land, when they can see nothing but sea."[1]

If you aren't seeing the possibilities, look a little deeper — or broader! Don't be distracted by the sea in front of your eyes. Remember the land you've seen, or imagine the land you haven't.

Lifetime Exercise: Positive Rescripting

If you want to find the best solutions to problems and problem people, if you want to be a better servant leader, be a more Agile person. Again, practice this in your mind by rescripting your real-life past encounters with difficult people — doing things more effectively this time around by applying the Five-Step Peace Process. This works even if you just apply the first three steps.

Rescripting is even more potent than using the stories in this book, and you can rescript and practice improving your skills as much as you want. Picture yourself effectively using Pause, Empathy, and Agility to rescript a situation with a difficult person.

Then, as soon as you are done, reboot your visualization and do it over and over, getting better and better at it. Turn this process into a skill and a personal strength.

Most people do some form of this after encountering difficult people, but they usually emphasize the negative or practice more effectively tearing down the other person. Instead, focus on being your best self and on coming up with better, more productive solutions. Be genuinely Agile!

Open your mind, as well as your eyes, and fill it with all sorts of new ideas and opportunities. People are amazing and capable of great things. Agility can help you figure out excellent, surprising solutions to difficult situations and people.

Consult with mentors, books, and audios to expand your thinking and creativity more. And to be even more effective at this, always look for how leaders deal with difficult people as you read, listen to audios, watch movies, or pay attention to other people in your life. Most of all, remember to approach any situation with Agility.

Before you act, always Pause, Empathize, and then use Agility to come up with the very best options—instead of just responding emotionally in the first way that comes to mind. This will make you powerful and greatly increase your success in life.

Workshop

Using the same process you did with the characters from the stories, analyze and consider some actual difficult people from your life. Get out a notebook, write a name at the top of the first sheet, and ask yourself questions. Then list some points about Empathy and Agility — actually write them down!

Take time for each of the steps, recording your thoughts and findings in your notebook as you go. This will give you some additional experience at using the process and might just supply some important ideas and answers to problems that you are currently dealing with.

STEP 4

Contribution

Legacy is not what's left tomorrow when you're gone.
It's what you give, create, impact and contribute
today while you're here that then happens to live on.
— RASHEED OGUNLARU

CHAPTER 21

Great Contribution

There are no words to express the abyss between
isolation and having one ally. It may be conceded to
the mathematician that four is twice two. But two is
not twice one; two is two thousand times one.
—G. K. CHESTERTON

In the Agility phase, we focused on opening up to all sorts of possibilities and considering many options and solutions. Agility is about getting creative, seeing the big picture, and broadening and deepening our vision so that no opportunity or excellent possibility falls through the cracks.

Contribution mode is essential because it is the point in the Five-Step Peace Process where leaders start cutting less-helpful possibilities and judging all options and possible responses to a difficult person by a very important measuring stick. Contribution is the narrowing-down phase. We've made a point of seeing everything. Now it's time to pick what's best and right for here and now.

Contribution is the standard by which top leaders judge possible solutions and select an actual plan of action. Because they have a long-term vision and have dedicated their lives to a powerful cause, top leaders know that their Contribution to situations and to the world is profoundly significant. They don't ignore the fact that their choices affect matters beyond themselves. In fact, they take this opportunity by the horns and make choices to determine what they want their impact to look like.

Contribution mode is where leaders ask themselves, "What does this all mean, and what *will* it mean in the long run?" By considering this question, they are able to determine what they want their Contribution to be, which is how they pick their response to the situation at hand.

Before they act, top leaders consider what to do not just in terms of consequences but also in terms of Contribution. It's not about *"How could this go wrong?"* but *"How does this fit into my life purpose, and what do I need to do in this moment or with this person to better further the mission?"*

This is Contribution.

Be Good for Something

Henry David Thoreau said, "Aim above morality. Be not *simply* good — be good for something."[1] The most successful and excellent people are those who have given their heart and soul to a cause that matters deeply. These are men and women who have, as top leader Orrin Woodward puts it, "thrown their hearts over the bar" and dedicated themselves to their God-given purpose.

This is what Contribution is all about. When people have such a vision of what life means to them, they don't leave it out of their decision-making process—even in a tense moment of dealing with a difficult person.

In fact, this life purpose is going to be one of the determining factors in pretty much everything they do, as it should be. Contribution mode is where top leaders look their life purpose full in the face and ask, in light of it, what should be done in this difficult moment.

Since the leaders have already considered their best self (Pause), the cares of the other person in the conversation (Empathy), and the possible solutions available in this difficulty (Agility), it is time to consider mission, impact, and legacy—what the leaders will Contribute *to* the situation.

It's not enough to just solve problems. Top leaders use difficult situations with difficult people as opportunities to improve matters—to Contribute in ways that last and make things genuinely better. Even if the difficult people reject this offer, the leaders are still at their best, and this will help them and others.

> *It's not enough to just solve problems. Top leaders use difficult situations with difficult people as opportunities to improve matters.*

Leaders who understand this principle and apply it in its proper place in the Five-Step Peace Process are so much more effective than people who don't because they're making a point of being effective—and not just in the short run or the small picture of one tense conversation with a difficult person. True Contribution is about making the small-picture choices that have the right big-picture impact.

The Personal Power of Living Intentionally

This comes down to being true to yourself, the best you. There's power in living intentionally for excellence.

If you don't remember your cause and life purpose in your decision-making and reacting process when faced with a difficult person, you've missed something vitally important. True leaders remember what they're fighting for so they can make every thrust, block, and parry count — and even choose *when* to utilize each!

Conscious Contribution matters greatly because some kind of Contribution is inevitable and unavoidable. All action has an impact. Those who actively seek Contribution in their interactions and dealings with people are living intentionally.

Those who consciously choose a good Contribution, even when faced by emotionally charged situations driven by difficult people, are true servant leaders, the ones who'll most effectively change the world for the better. In fact, the Contribution phase is the point in the inner dialogue of Pause where top leaders ensure the right kind of change, impact, allies, and legacy.

Those who choose to make a positive Contribution don't just deal with difficult people; they naturally make allies, and they change the world for good, one difficult person at a time!

CHAPTER 22

Contribute Self: What to Be Instead of Difficult

The sweetest pleasure arises from difficulties overcome.
— PUBLIUS SYRUS

The Contribution phase is a great time for leaders to refocus on who and what they want to be, since being difficult themselves has already been ruled out as an option. You've heard the sayings that nature abhors a vacuum, that it's easier to replace a habit than to simply stop a habit, and that you can't get something for nothing.

When it comes to what kind of person to be in a tough situation, it's more effective to focus on what you want to be than on what you don't want to be. You know you shouldn't be difficult, but what *should* you be?

Filling the Vacuum

There is something that works much better than just fighting against your emotional desire to lash out at a difficult person or, at the opposite extreme, caving in out of cowardice. Define the kind of person you really want to be—with specific comparisons to the behavior or character quality you're avoiding—and spend some time and energy developing the attributes and habits that go along with this defined "excellent character."

While it's important not to be difficult, it's actually even better—and a lot more productive—to be truly and fantastically outstanding. Chris Brady suggests that since we tend to reflect back what we are, the solution to the whole not-being-a-difficult-person conundrum is to "develop and earn a reputation of fairness."[1]

The key phrase here is "develop and earn." Your goal is not just to *seem* fair. It's to genuinely *be* fair. As prospective leaders make a point of being aboveboard in all their dealings, people start to notice. Soon even their worst enemies will know who they are and what they stand for.

Rather than being difficult, or even just trying not to be difficult, what if you were a remarkable, top-notch individual? What if you used Pause, Empathy, Agility, and Contribution in all your interactions with people—not just difficult ones, but *every* one?

You know you don't want to be difficult. (You really don't want that yucky smell in your nose wherever you go.) But now ask yourself, "What do I want to be instead of difficult? What will I choose to replace the difficulty that used to be me?" In part, this is the Contribution leaders make to the discussion: the Contribution of an excellent self.

Make note of anything that popped into your mind when you asked yourself these questions, and add it to your list of skills and personal traits to develop. In the meantime, we have a few additional ideas for you.

Be Honest, Reliable, and Consistent

It's pretty difficult to deal with someone who is not honest, reliable, and consistent. Aesop taught, "A doubtful friend is worse than a certain enemy. Let a man be one thing or the other, and we then know how to meet him."[2] Frankly, people who settle for being a "doubtful friend" are generally lumped into the "enemy" category anyway because you can't depend on them.

When someone isn't an honest, reliable, and consistent person, first of all, people will know it, and second, they'll tend to define the relationship with such a person accordingly.

By contrast, as a person develops these qualities and creates a history of faithfully exhibiting them, she'll become the kind of individual others can trust, respect, love, and count on. Moreover, people will *know* that this is the kind of person they're dealing with.

This is absolutely vital to success at not being difficult, and it also happens to matter a whole lot in success as a friend, leader, and person.

Keep Emotional Control

The kind of person who's constantly losing it emotionally and whose associates tend to describe him as "out of control" should take it as a pretty big clue that he is being a difficult person and not the kind of person he ought to be.

We're not trying to pick on anyone who has any of these weaknesses. We're merely pointing out that the strengths on the flip side of them are traits a person really ought to strive for if he is going to be a success in life, especially in dealing with difficult people.

We understand that all people have moments when they get upset and sometimes even lose their temper and emotional control. We're just suggesting that rather than being okay with that, a good approach to life is taking responsibility for such failures and genuinely doing your best to remain in emotional control of yourself. It's really as simple as making a habit of Pause in your life.

As Dorian in Oscar Wilde's *The Picture of Dorian Gray* said, "I don't want to be at the mercy of my emotions. I want to use them, to enjoy them, and to dominate them."[3] People who are at the mercy of their emotions are rarely as reliable, consistent, or dependable as those who have mastered their emotions. For this reason and others, they tend to be a lot more difficult themselves and a lot less effective at dealing with difficult people or anything else they set out to do.

So strive to develop and maintain emotional control. Use Pause. It is extremely effective. Be the boss of yourself, rather than allowing your fickle emotions to run the show. As you do this, you'll be a lot better at exemplifying the other traits of great leaders, and you'll also be a lot less difficult for other people to deal with.

Firm and Courageous, Likable and Forgiving

This is pretty simple and can be handled in a few sentences. A Contribution-minded person seeks to be the kind of individual who stands up for what she believes in but doesn't go out of her way to smash people who disagree with her. She doesn't play the Boss or the Autocrat or even the Bureaucrat. Such a person makes a point of letting her stand on principle be known, without trying to shove it down people's throats.

It is important to be strong in pursuing and performing your mission, but it's also a good idea to make some friends and allies along the way. As Winston Churchill famously declared, "Courage is what it takes to stand up and speak; courage is also what it takes to sit down and listen."[4] To be an effective leader, you have to become good at both.

The people you interact with should know you as a person who justly does both of these. Be the kind of leader who doesn't hesitate to reprimand with love when needed but who is also quick to forgive when that time comes. Also, be the kind of leader who gives out a lot of praise — much more than any kind of reproof.

Be firm and courageous, likable and forgiving. Be fun and full of genuine praise. As you develop these habits and this reputation among the people you work with, your ability to influence, serve, and deal with them will grow significantly as their trust in your opinion and character deepens.

When you are such a person all the time, encounters with difficult people are easier—because you are naturally at your best right from the beginning. Pause is simple because it is your daily habit. The same is true of Empathy and Agility. And you naturally seek positive Contribution to help the difficult person—without getting easily caught up in the emotional storm of protecting a self-centered ego.

As you live trying to be a servant leader, you are practicing for the times when a difficult person comes along.

Don't Be Judgmental, Assign Motives, or Gossip

Finally, as you make a point of never doing hurtful and backbiting things—of not being judgmental, assigning motives, or gossiping—you'll be cultivating a habit and reputation of fairness. You'll be a leader of character who works well with people. When people know you're fair, they tend to be a lot less difficult in general, and they want to work *with* you rather than against you or around you.

In short, when you've got people dedicated to working with you, you've won half the battle of dealing with difficult people because you're actually working *with* them (versus emotionally responding *to* them) and your example often inspires others to try to be less difficult themselves.

Better Is...Better

In summary, make a point of being *not* difficult and of being a stellar example of what you wish all the difficult people in your life would be. Do this not only because it will often inspire others to be less difficult but because it's the whole point!

The goal isn't really to be "not difficult"; it's to be truly excellent.

As we said before, do this because it's the person you want to be! Your influence and impact will be much greater when you're a person who is

> *The goal isn't really to be "not difficult"; it's to be truly excellent.*

striving for excellence. In doing this, remember you're Contributing something that's truly invaluable—your best self.

This is the first Contribution every prospective leader should seek to give, day in and day out, because without it, any further Contribution will be much smaller, if not entirely meaningless.

CHAPTER 23

Contribution and Winning

It is deeply satisfying to win a prize.
—FROM CHARLOTTE'S WEB BY E. B. WHITE

In *The 7 Habits of Highly Effective People*,[1] Stephen Covey taught the important leadership principle of seeking win–win solutions to problems and interactions. A win–win solution is one where both parties come out of the interaction feeling that they won. Their needs have been met, they have been taken care of, and they are happy with the outcome of the situation.

The combination of Empathy and Contribution very clearly supports this idea, and top leaders understand how powerful and useful it is to find win–win answers. Since, as David Schwartz taught, the other person in the scenario is important and you are too, win–win is obviously the best result when it can be achieved.

This is one of the reasons Agility is so important—to consider all the possible ways to end up with the best scenario for everyone involved.

Jack Campbell said, "You can't win unless you try to win."[2] Those who never seek a situation that leaves everyone in the happy, triumphant, and fulfilled state of a real winner will likely never achieve it. One of the best Contributions a leader can make to a situation and to his cause in general is a true win–win answer to any conflicts or difficult people who come at him.

This isn't always possible because the difficult person may not want a win–win, but you can always at least offer such an outcome. To do this, during the Agility phase, leaders look in particular for the options and solutions that will allow such a happy ending to the conflict, struggle, and strife that often accompanies difficult people.

In reality, the entire Peace Process so far has been pointing to a win–win resolution whenever possible. Pause and Empathy clearly recommend it, Agility reveals possible ways to obtain it, and Contribution is almost always greater when both sides win.

That said, top leaders seek to Contribute with a win–win scenario whenever they can pull it off without compromising what is right.

Contribute a Win–Lose

A win–win situation is a fantastic Contribution, and top leaders seek it whenever possible. But there is a significant difference between Covey's "Think Win/Win" and the true essence of the principle of Contribution.

Effective leaders seeking to make a positive Contribution understand that win–win is good when it's right, but they aren't afraid to pursue a win–lose when this is needed in service to the right values. This only happens when the difficult person in the situation refuses the win–win options.

Successful, Contribution-driven people know that sometimes, as Robin Hobb put it, "The fight isn't over until you win."[3] As a leader, you have to be willing to fight for the right, even when it could hurt other people's feelings. You shouldn't seek to hurt others or cause difficulty for them, but top leaders do not cower or cave in on key principles just because they want to reconcile, avoid conflict, or make other people happy at any cost.

In seeking Contribution, leaders must not forget about Empathy and Agility, but they absolutely must be willing to put the right Contribution above matters of lesser meaning and importance.

> *Leaders do not cower or cave in on key principles just because they want to reconcile, avoid conflict, or make other people happy at any cost.*

Leaders should be clear on what's wrong in the situation and why it's wrong and act accordingly. Sometimes the best way to handle difficult people, the way that Contributes the most, is to put distance between them and you—or to stop them if their difficultness escalates too far.

Sometimes you just flat-out have to get rid of people for the good of the team, company, and so on. Steve Sample wrote about this concept of "one good kill to save the herd" in his book *The Contrarian's Guide to Leadership*.[4]

There may come a time when you've done all you can do without sacrificing parts of your mission or life purpose, and you break fellowship. There is a time to fire people, walk away, show them the door, or tell them to their face that they don't get what they want because it's selfish, wrong, or against the purpose of the team. There are even times for legal action. With all such escalations, it is even more important to go through the proper steps of Pause, Empathy, and Agility.

When it is time to make such difficult decisions, be sure to act with love but also with courage. Top leaders remember their purpose and don't let anything stand in the way, no matter how much they seek to be "nice." And as mentioned, they do spend a lot of their time working to be nice.

> *Act with love but also with courage.*

People who understand success and greatness are willing to give their all to a win–lose situation when it's right. To paraphrase what Thomas Jefferson wrote in the Declaration of Independence, they should of course try out the win–win options first. This is absolutely vital to true success in dealing with difficult people and in life.

Those who aren't willing to sacrifice relationships, feelings, and difficulties for the good of their life mission and to do the right thing need to rethink their priorities or content themselves with less-than-worthy service to their true friends, family, dreams, goals, and cause.

The point is not to be selfish, callous, or mean, but real leaders simply do not enslave themselves to the whims of difficult people. They don't enter relationships, engagements, or commitments where there is obvious, consistent, systemic bad behavior on

> *Real leaders simply do not enslave themselves to the whims of difficult people.*

display, and they aren't afraid to remedy the situation when it's their responsibility and stewardship to do so. As Chris Brady said, "It's one thing to serve them; it's another to hitch your wagon to theirs."[5] In short, leaders do not allow their cause to fail because they were too afraid to let its opponents and enemies lose.

It's All about the Cause

This is heavy content, and we understand that it can be difficult to practice. Remember, leaders should seek to deal with people with love, patience, Pause, and Empathy. This is not about eating people with your cause or using the Five-Step Peace Process to justify hurting people unnecessarily or becoming any sort of difficult person yourself.

It is important not to let this principle turn into justification of bad or ego-driven behavior. Leaders must combine love and courage with wisdom here, not just go around whacking people with their dauntless courage alone. And they should give concerted effort to Agility; often effective solutions and compromises can be found with enough care and effort.

But there is also a time to take a stand. In fact, if you're the type of person who tends more toward hurting your cause by being too confrontational, inconsiderate, undiplomatic, or tactless, this message is for you as well. Remember that Contribution to the cause comes first, even if this requires you to change yourself.

Brady went on to say, "Everyone tends one way or the other—courage or love—so whichever one you tend toward, take extra care to include the other in your dealings. They are the most important two things when it comes to dealing with difficult people and situations."[6]

> *"Everyone tends one way or the other— courage or love—so whichever one you tend toward, take extra care to include the other in your dealings. They are the most important two things when it comes to dealing with difficult people and situations."*
> —Chris Brady

Contribution is all about the cause, and if the cause matters, it is a battle—because difficult people will always show up to fight against things that really matter.

Top leaders love and respect people enough to seek happiness and success for others. They often serve and sacrifice to help people achieve these. But what they don't do—what they mustn't do, for the sake of their cause—is allow a desire to be kind to their enemies to cost them the cause itself.

To put it bluntly, leaders who understand Contribution do not allow the difficulty of others to stand in the way of their success, their dreams, and their cause. They love people, they serve people, and they help people in all the ways they can. But they do it to strengthen their true and real purpose, never to avoid conflict, difficulty, or courage.

And of course, they also don't let their tendency to be too abrupt, thoughtless, or insensitive when it comes to other people's needs and feelings get in the way of accomplishing their mission.

Give It All!

Contribution is about considering the cause you were born to live for and being willing to make every sort of sacrifice—from personal comfort to unhealthy relationships—in order to do your best to fulfill your role in the world. Those who genuinely do this will live happier lives and do more for the good of the world than those who don't.

This deeply matters, and it is one of the most important aspects of dealing with difficult people. Work very hard to seek win–win solutions, using Agility to creatively find them even when they are extremely difficult, but know when it is time to choose the cause and take a stand. Without this, there is no real leadership.

To summarize: When a difficult person crosses your path, first Pause and make sure you respond as your best self. Second, use Empathy to really understand what the difficult person is going through and what he or she truly needs. Third, use Agility and innovative, out-of-the-ordinary thinking to brainstorm a number of possible options to fix the problem. Fourth, decide which choice will bring the very best results, and Contribute your best self, ideas, attitude, and principled treatment of the difficult person to the situation. Whether or not the difficult person accepts your win–win options, you will at least be at your best during the whole experience.

Stand for what's right, and be creative and open-minded as you seek the most effective solutions. As you do this, whenever possible, find a way to help the difficult person.

STEP 5

Epiphany

Small things start us in new ways of thinking.

—V. S. NAIPAUL

CHAPTER 24

Eureka!

*Far better it is to dare mighty things, to win glorious triumphs,
even though checkered by failure, than to take rank with those
poor spirits who neither enjoy much nor suffer much, because
they live in the gray twilight that knows not victory nor defeat.*
— THEODORE ROOSEVELT

Epiphany is the smallest piece of the Five-Step Peace Process — but not for any lack of importance. In fact, while it usually takes the least time and actual work, it is in many ways the pinnacle of the process.

The reason you go through Steps 1 – 4 is to prepare yourself to experience and enact Step 5. Dean C. Ross said, "[W]ithout the quest there can be no epiphany,"[1] which is absolutely true. But make no mistake, the goal of the quest is to get to an Epiphany.

You can call it Epiphany or something else, but whether you name it "Aha!" or "Eureka!" or "Inspiration," it is a vital part of the Five-Step Peace Process and a valuable secret to dealing with difficult people.

Epiphany Uncovered

Just what is this special thing we call Epiphany? It comes at the point after all your Pausing, consideration, and deliberation when that perfect light bulb brightens in your head, and you know what to do to handle the situation. Sometimes it takes more time, prayer, thought, and reflection to get there than others, but until Epiphany strikes, the "thought and deliberation" part of your journey isn't quite over yet.

When you receive a stroke of genius seemingly from nowhere, the real solution comes. But it takes work to get there. Pause, Empathy, innovative Agility, and positive Contribution are your part of dealing with difficult people, and when you do these, Epiphany can naturally strike.

Epiphany seldom comes when you are sitting around waiting for the right idea to magically appear in front of you so you'll be able to miraculously tie things up in a pretty pink bow. Not at all. Top leaders understand that as they pay the price to understand the situation and the problem and then work hard to find the right solutions, win–win if at all possible, they really will find the answers they seek, often in ways that feel miraculous, surprising, even heaven-sent.

This is a powerful principle of leadership, and it is extremely important when it comes to dealing with difficult people (and problem solving in general). Working hard to understand and find the solutions to a problem really does pay off when you know the right steps and look with proper vision.

Epiphany is not only potent; it is the highest goal of the Five-Step Peace Process. As leaders go through the other four steps and gain a deep and profound understanding of everything at work within the situation, they're setting themselves up to receive a beautiful blast of wisdom on how to react. This hardly ever happens without Pause. And it is more likely to happen when Pause is combined with Empathy, Agility, and Contribution.

Put most simply, Epiphany is the natural result of following the other four steps. When you take powerful action to Pause, employ Empathy, think with Agility, and positively Contribute, something happens. In addition to improving your reactions, you also begin to have better, brighter ideas. The right kind of action leads to more effective and creative thinking. This is Epiphany.

Predictable Miracles

This is a powerful concept, so use it! Go through the steps in the process so you'll be ready to meet Epiphany when it comes, and keep your eyes and ears wide open for the answers that are waiting to present themselves to you at the most opportune moment. Epiphany usually comes only when you are working hard to do your part, from Pause to positive Contribution and everything in between.

Once you capture and leverage the power of Epiphany, you'll be solving problems, dealing with difficult people in interesting and effective (and even surprising) ways, and making more exciting Contributions to the world.

Epiphany is real, but it isn't hit or miss. It comes naturally, even predictably, at the right time once you've done your best to apply the previous four steps. When you do your part, great ideas will come to you.

CHAPTER 25

Epiphany →
Innovation

If you want to teach people a new way of thinking, don't
bother trying to teach them. Instead, give them a tool,
the use of which will lead to new ways of thinking.
—R. Buckminster Fuller

Bryant McGill said, "People have moments of consciousness and epiphanies throughout their lives, but then suppress the realization."[1] For the Five-Step Peace Process to work, it is important that genuine Epiphany leads to just as genuine action.

In fact, the power of Epiphany is that it inevitably leads to authentic and dynamic innovation. Top leaders who go through the Five-Step Peace Process and arrive at Epiphany automatically transition from Epiphany to innovation.

The whole process, ending with Epiphany, is meant to serve as a launching pad from difficulty to innovation. Stimulus (difficulty) leads to response (effective innovation). When dealing with a difficult person, this is incredibly powerful.

This process makes sense because true Epiphany leaves you with exactly what you need to powerfully innovate in whatever situation or area of life you find yourself. Thus, Pause is essentially about taking a moment to allow for the process of innovation.

Empathy, Agility, and Contribution are meant to give you the information to achieve Epiphany, and Epiphany leads to innovation. Real innovation, life-changing innovation that alters the equation and shifts the world, is the culmination of the whole concept and exactly what leaders are looking to achieve through leveraging the moments between stimulus and response.

In this way, getting to innovation is the responsibility of those who would be leaders. It is also their goal. When innovation is the goal and you choose the right steps to get to it (the five steps), you will be able to take effective initiative and consistently make inspired and ingenious changes in everything you touch. This is invaluable in dealing with difficult people and situations.

This truly works. It is simple, elegant, and profound. It is real. But it only works if you Pause and then apply the other steps of the process. None of these steps is difficult, but without them, you lose your power to lead. When you do apply the steps of the Peace Process, you have the skill to move events always in the best direction possible.

You don't have to bring Epiphany. In fact, the harder you try, the less likely it is to come. Your role is first to Pause and then to engage Empathy, Agility, and Contribution. Epiphany will take care of itself if you do the other four steps. Then, when great ideas do come, act on them. This turns difficulty into innovation and dealing with difficult people into innovative leadership.

This is extremely effective in dealing with difficult people and in facing numerous other challenges as well. This process is vital wisdom for top leaders.

Specific Applications

If you want something new, you have to stop doing something old.
—PETER F. DRUCKER

In addition to knowing the seven main types of difficult people and employing the Five-Step Peace Process, there are a few practical guidelines that will help you deal with difficult people. These are simple and straightforward enough to be listed as bullet points, but they are extremely important.

Practical considerations include the following:

- Never get involved in any controversy through voice mail, e-mail, etc. Do it face-to-face. This is imperative, even if distance is a concern. Words frequently get taken out of context in electronic communications, and they can be used against you later. Meet in person to address or deal with any difficulty.

- If you have a choice in the matter, don't entangle yourself with someone through a commitment when obvious bad behavior is consistently exhibited. This is true with:
  - o   Hiring and being hired
  - o   Roommates
  - o   Project partners
  - o   Business partnership
  - o   Marriage (especially!)
  - o   Other lasting partnerships

  In some instances, the best way to deal with difficult people is to put distance between them and you. Don't allow them into your life, if possible.

- Always gravitate toward more productive, harmonious, character-based people. Just like negativity can (and nearly always does) spread in relationships and groups, so can positive, leadership-oriented attitudes and behaviors. Choose your partners wisely.
- If you are in authority, make sure you document correctly and all along the way.
- Let the difficult person know you are documenting.
- Always attack the behavior, not the person.
- Have another party as a witness.
- Fire sooner rather than later if it's obvious that major problems will not be resolved.
- Remember that how you address the bottom 10 percent (especially consistently difficult people) has a major influence on how the middle 80 percent

choose to act. (The top 10 percent will always do well but will still appreciate it that you appropriately responded to the "slackers.")

Conclusion

You are going to face difficult people. We all are. How we respond, especially in the first few seconds after the difficulty arrives — when we choose to Pause or not to Pause — has a huge impact on what kind of people and leaders we become and how much success we can experience.

Top leaders learn to deal with difficult people effectively, humanely, creatively, and with an eye toward excellence. They operate from a position of strength and self-control because they learn to master the Five-Step Peace Process and the simple, practical basics of effectively dealing with difficult people.

Now that you've learned how to do this, use your new wisdom. Deal well with difficult people, and you'll improve the quality and success of your leadership.

The mind that opens to a new
idea never returns to its original size.
— ALBERT EINSTEIN

NOTES

INTRODUCTION

1   Marcus Aurelius, *The Essential Marcus Aurelius*, Tarcher Cornerstone Editions, translated and introduced by Jacob Needleman and John P. Piazza (New York: Jeremy P. Tarcher/ Penguin, 2008), p. 86.

PART ONE

CHAPTER 1

1   Walt Disney Productions, *Peter Pan*, based on the play *Peter Pan, or the Boy Who Wouldn't Grow Up* by J. M. Barrie, screenplay by Milt Banta, WilliamCottrell, Winston Hibler, Bill Peet, Erdman Penner, Joe Rinaldi, Ted Sears, and Ralph Wright, released February 5, 1953, directed by Clyde Geronimi, Wilfred Jackson, and Hamilton Luske, produced by Walt Disney.

2   *Cinderella*, a European folk tale by A. Anderson published in *Histoires ou contes du temps passé* by Charles Perrault in 1697 an in *Grimms' Fairy Tales* by the Brothers Grimm that has formed the basis of many notable works in theatre, opera, ballet, songs, television, and film, including the most well-known film adaptation from Walt Disney Productions released February 15, 1950.

3   Charles Lutwidge Dodgson (under the pseudonym Lewis Carroll), *Alice's Adventures in Wonderland* (London: Macmillan and Co., 1865).

CHAPTER 2

1   Jane Austen, *Pride and Prejudice* (London: T. Egerton, Whitehall, 1813).

2   Lucy Maud Montgomery, *Anne of Green Gables* (Boston: L.C. Page and Co., 1908).

3   *Jingle All the Way*, screenplay by Randy Kornfield, directed by Brian Levant, produced by Chris Columbus, Michael Barnathan, and Mark Radcliffe, 1492 Pictures, distributed by 20th Century Fox, released November 3, 1998, United States.

CHAPTER 3

1   Victor Hugo, *Les Misérables* (Bruxelles: A. Lacroix, Verboeckhoven & Cie., 1862).

2   Rick Berman, Michael Piller, and Jeri Taylor, *Star Trek: Voyager*, television series based on the original *Star Trek* series by Gene Roddenberry, released January 16, 1995 and aired from 1995 to 2001, produced by Paramount Television, United Paramount Network (UPN), United States.

3   Walt Disney Productions, *The Little Mermaid*, film directed by Ron Clements and John Musker, produced by John Musker and Howard Ashman, screenplay by Ron Clements and John Musker, story by John Musker, Ron Clements, Howard Ashman, Gerrit Graham, Sam Graham, and Chris Hubbell, based on the fairy tale *The Little Mermaid* by Hans Christian Andersen, released November 17, 1989, United States.

CHAPTER 4

1   Alan Alexander Milne, *Winnie-the-Pooh* (London: Methuen & Co. Ltd., 1926).

CHAPTER 5

1   Malcolm Gladwell, *Outliers: The Story of Success* (New York: Little, Brown and Company, 2008).

2   Chris Brady, *Rascal: Making a Difference by Becoming an Original Character* (Flint, MI: Obstaclés Press, 2010).

3   Harriet Beecher Stowe, *Uncle Tom's Cabin; or, Life among the Lowly* (Boston: John P. Jewett & Company / Cleveland, OH: Jewett, Proctor & Worthington, 1852).

4   Clive Staples Lewis, *The Chronicles of Narnia*, series of seven novels written between 1949 and 1954, originally published in London by HarperCollins between October 16, 1950 and September 4, 1956.

5   Brady, *Rascal*.

CHAPTER 6

1   Superman is a character created by Jerry Siegel and Joe Shuster who first appeared in *Action Comics* #1, published April 18, 1938 (cover-dated June 1938) by DC Comics (owned by Time Warner and headquartered in Burbank, CA).

2   Austen, *Pride and Prejudice*.

CHAPTER 7

1   Austen, *Pride and Prejudice*.

2   John Ronald Reuel Tolkien, *The Lord of the Rings*, novel written in stages between 1937 and 1949 and published in three volumes (*The Fellowship of the Ring*, July 29, 1954; *The Two Towers*, November 11, 1954; and *The Return of the King*, October 20, 1955) by George Allen & Unwin, United Kingdom.

PART TWO

1　　Sun Tzu, *The Art of War: The Oldest Military Treatise in the World (VIII: Variation in Tactics)*, translated from the Chinese by Lionel Giles, M.A. (London: Luzac & Co., 1910).

CHAPTER 8

1　　Viktor Frankl, *Man's Search for Meaning: An Introduction to Logotherapy* (first English translation was titled *From Death-Camp to Existentialism*), translated by Ilse Lasch (Vienna, Austria: Verlag für Jugend und Volk, 1946 / Boston, United States: Beacon Press, 1959.

2　　Kevin Cashman, *The Pause Principle* (Berrett-Koehler Publishers, 2012).

3　　Ibid.

CHAPTER 9

1　　Chris Brady, "Dealing with Difficult People (LLR 602)," speech given in Salt Lake City, UT, on July 13, 2014, audio recording released on November 1, 2014 (Flint, MI: LIFE Leadership, 2013).

2　　Ibid.

3　　Mark Twain, *The Complete Works of Mark Twain: Mark Twain's Notebook* (New York: Harper and Brothers, 1935), p. 393.

CHAPTER 10

1　　"Quotations by Albert Einstein," *The MacTutor History of Mathematics Archive*, created by John J. O'Connor and Edmund F. Robertson, February 2006, School of Mathematics and Statistics, University of St. Andrews, Scotland, http://www-history.mcs.st-andrews.ac.uk/Quotations/Einstein.html.

CHAPTER 11

1　　A Lincoln Library, "Abraham Lincoln Quotes," http://www.alincoln-library.com/abraham-lincoln-quotes.shtml, accessed July 14, 2014.

CHAPTER 12

1   David Schwartz, *The Magic of Thinking Big* (Fireside, 1987), p. 56.

2   Landon Palmer, "Year in Review: How Movies in 2013 Were about Becoming Somebody Else," *Culture Warrior*, posted December 31, 2013, *Film School Rejects*, copyright 2006-2014 Reject Media, LLC, filmschoolrejects.com/tag/empathy.

CHAPTER 13

1   Stephen Covey, *The 7 Habits of Highly Effective People* (New York: Free Press, div. of Simon & Schuster, 1989).

CHAPTER 14

1   Benjamin Chase "Ben" Harper, "Never Leave Lonely Alone," *Both Sides of the Gun* (2 x CD), released March 20, 2006, record label Virgin Records America, United Kingdom.

2   Andrea Boutelle, "The Authentic Advocate: Ashley Judd," February 18, 2014, copyright 2014, The Women's Fund of Central Ohio, womensfundcentralohio.org/tag/advocacy.

3   John C. Maxwell, *Relationships 101* (Nashville, TN: Thomas Nelson Inc., 2003).

CHAPTER 15

1   Mark Frost, *The Grand Slam: Bobby Jones, America, and the Story of Golf* (Hyperion, 2004), 197.

CHAPTER 16

1   William Barrett, *The Illusion of Technique: A Search for Meaning in a Technological Civilization* (Anchor Press, 1979).

CHAPTER 19

1   Albert Einstein, "Albert Einstein Quotes," facts.co, einsteinquotes.facts.co/alberteinsteinquotesby/einsteainquotes.php, accessed July 14, 2014.

2   Christyne (chan6es), "Change Is Me: Who Said Progress Is Impossible without Change?," October 23, 2012 at 10:03 a.m., chan6es.me/2012/10/23/who-said-progress-is-impossible-without-change/.

3   Marcus Aurelius, *Meditations*, Book 6, verse 21 (New York: Penguin Group Inc. Classics, 2006), p. 50.

CHAPTER 20

1   Francis Bacon, *The Advancement of Learning*, Book II, vii, 5 (New York: Modern Library, Division of Random House, 2001), p. 98.

CHAPTER 21

1   Henry David Thoreau, Letter to Harrison Gray Otis Blake, March 27, 1848, *The Correspondence: The Writings of Henry D. Thoreau, Volume 1: 1834 – 1848*, Edited by Robert N. Hudspeth (Princeton, NJ: Princeton University Press, 2013), p. 362.

CHAPTER 22

1   Brady, "Dealing with Difficult People."

2   A. Jay Adler, "The 'Peace and Justice' Charade," June 4, 2012, 11:32 a.m., *The Times of Isreal*, copyright 2014, blogs.timesofisreal.com/the-peace-and-justice-charade/.

3   Oscar Wilde, *The Picture of Dorian Gray and Other Writings* (New York: Pocket Books, 2005), p. 117.

4   Winston Churchill, Speech at a conference in Washington DC, as quoted in *The Imperfect State: An American Odyssey* by John Barron (Indianapolis, IN: Dog Ear Publishing, 2010), p. 560.

CHAPTER 23

1   Covey, *The 7 Habits of Highly Effective People.*

2   Jack Campbell, *The Lost Fleet: Relentless* (London: Titan Books, 2009).

3   Robin Hobb, *The Farseer: Royal Assassin*, Book 2 of the Trilogy (New York: Spectra, 1997).

4   Steve Sample, *The Contrarian's Guide to Leadership* (San Francisco, CA: Jossey-Bass, 2002).

5   Brady, "Dealing with Difficult People."

6   Ibid.

CHAPTER 24

1   Dean C. Ross, *Reflections on a Simple Twist of Fate: Literature, Art and Parinson's Disease* (Katonah, New York, 2011), p. 196.

CHAPTER 25

1   Bryant McGill, "Lust for Possession, Greed and Post-Human, Consumer Hedonism," copyright 2014 Bryant McGill, bryantmcgill.com/20131201130606.html.

Other Books in the
LIFE Leadership Essentials Series

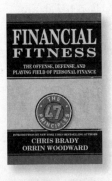

Financial Fitness: The Offense, Defense, and Playing Field of Personal Finance with Introduction by Chris Brady and Orrin Woodward – $21.95
If you ever feel that you're too far behind and can't envision a better financial picture, you are so WRONG! You need this book! The *Financial Fitness* book is for everyone at any level of wealth. Just like becoming physically or mentally fit, becoming financially fit requires two things: knowing what to do and taking the necessary action to do it. Learn how to prosper, conserve, and become fiscally fantastic. It's a money thing, and the power to prosper is all yours!

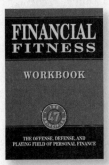

Financial Fitness Workbook – $7.95
Economic affairs don't have to be boring or stressful. Make managing money fun in a few simple steps. Use this workbook to get off to a great start and then continue down the right path to becoming fiscally fabulous! Discover exactly where all of your money actually goes as you make note of all your expenditures. Every page will put you one step closer to financial freedom, so purchase the *Financial Fitness Workbook* today and get budgeting!

Mentoring Matters: Targets, Techniques, and Tools for Becoming a Great Mentor with Foreword by Orrin Woodward – $19.95
Get your sticky notes ready for all the info you're about to take in from this book. Do you know what it means to be a *great* mentor? It's a key part of successful leadership, but for most people, the necessary skills and techniques don't come naturally. Educate yourself on all of the key targets, techniques, and tools for becoming a magnificent mentor with this easy-to-apply manual. Your leadership success will be forever increased!

Turn the Page: How to Read Like a Top Leader with **Introduction by Chris Brady – $15.95**
Leaders are readers. But there are many ways to read, and leaders read differently than most people do. They read to learn what they need to know, do, or feel, regardless of the author's intent or words. They see past the words and read with the specific intent of finding truth and applying it directly in their own lives. Learn how to read like a top leader so you'll be better able to emulate their success. Applying the skills taught in *Turn the Page* will impact your life, career, and leadership abilities in ways you can't even imagine. So turn the page and start reading!

SPLASH!: A Leader's Guide to Effective Public Speaking with **Foreword by Chris Brady – $15.95**
For many, the fear of giving a speech is worse than the fear of death. But public speaking can be truly enjoyable *and* a powerful tool for making a difference in the lives of others. Whether you are a beginner or a seasoned orator, this book will help you transform your public speaking to a whole new level of leadership influence. Learn the SPLASH formula for great public speaking that will make you the kind of speaker and leader who makes a SPLASH—leaving any audience, big or small, forever changed—every time you speak!

The Serious Power of Fun with **Foreword by Chris Brady – $15.95**
Life got you down? Feeling like life isn't much fun is a bad place to be. Fun matters. It is serious business and a source of significant leadership power. Without it, few people maintain the levels of inspired motivation and sustained effort that bring great success. So put a smile back on your face. Discover how to make every area of life more enjoyable and turn any situation into the right kind of fun. Learn to cultivate a habit of designed gratification—where life just keeps getting better—and *laugh your way to increased success* with *The Serious Power of Fun!*

Wavemakers: How Small Acts of Courage Can Change the World with Foreword by Chris Brady – $15.95
Every now and then, extraordinary individuals come along who make huge waves and bring about permanent change in the lives of so many that society as a whole is forever altered. Discover from the examples of the various "Wavemakers" showcased in this book how you can make waves of your own and change the world for the better!

Subscriptions and Products from
LIFE Leadership

Rascal Radio Subscription – $49.95 per month
Rascal Radio by LIFE Leadership is the world's first online personal development radio hot spot. Rascal Radio is centered on LIFE Leadership's 8 Fs: Faith, Family, Finances, Fitness, Following, Freedom, Friends, and Fun. Subscribers have unlimited access to **hundreds and hundreds** of audio recordings that they can stream endlessly from both the **LIFE Leadership website** and the **LIFE Leadership Smartphone App.** Listen to one of the preset stations or customize your own based on speaker or subject. Of course, you can easily skip tracks or "like" as many as you want. And if you are listening from the website, you can purchase any one of these incredible audios.

Let Rascal Radio provide you with **life-changing information to help you live the life you've always wanted!**

The LIFE Series – $50.00 per month
Here's where LIFE Leadership began—with the now famously followed 8 Fs: Family, Finances, Fitness, Faith, Following, Freedom, Friends, and Fun. This highly recommended series offers a strong foundation on which to build and advance in every area of your daily life. The timeless truths and effective strategies included will reignite passion and inspire you to be your very best. Transform your life for the better and watch how it will create positive change in the lives of those around you. Subscribe today and have the time of your LIFE!

Series includes 4 audios and 1 book monthly and is also available in Spanish and French.

The LLR (Launching a Leadership Revolution) Series – $50.00 per month

There is no such thing as a born leader. Based on the *New York Times* bestseller *Launching a Leadership Revolution* by Chris Brady and Orrin Woodward, this series focuses on teaching leadership skills at every level. The principles and specifics taught in the LLR Series will equip you with all the tools you need for business advancement, community influence, church impact, and even an advantage in your home life. Topics include: leadership, finances, public speaking, goal setting,

mentoring, game planning, accountability and tracking of progress, levels of motivation and influence, and leaving a personal legacy. Will you be ready to take the lead when you're called? Subscribe now and learn how to achieve effective confidence skills while growing stronger in your leadership ability.

Series includes 4 audios and 1 leadership book monthly.

The AGO (All Grace Outreach) Series – $25.00 per month

We are all here together to love one another and take care of each other. But sometimes in this hectic world, we lose our way and forget our true purpose. When you subscribe to the AGO Series, you'll gain the valuable support and guidance that every Christian searches for. Nurture your soul, strengthen your faith, and find answers to better understand God's plan for your life, marriage, and children.

Series includes 1 audio and 1 book monthly.

The Edge Series – $10.00 per month
You'll cut in front of the rest of the crowd when you get the *Edge*. Designed for those on the younger side of life, this hard-core, no-frills series promotes self-confidence, drive, and motivation. Get advice, timely information, and true stories of success from interesting talks and fascinating people. Block out the noise around you and learn the principles of self-improvement at an early age. It's a gift that will keep on giving from parent to child. Subscribe today and get a competitive *Edge* on tomorrow.
  Series includes 1 audio monthly.

Financial Fitness Subscription – $10.00 per month for 12 months
If you found the *Financial Fitness Pack* life-changing and beneficial to your bank account, then you'll want even more timely information and guidance from the Financial Fitness Subscription. It's designed as a continuing economic education to help people develop financial discipline and overall knowledge of how their money works. Learn how to make financial principles your financial habits. It's a money thing, and it always pays to be cash savvy.
  Subscription includes 1 audio monthly.

**Financial Fitness Pack –
$99.99**

Once and for all, it's time to free yourself from the worry and heavy burden of debt. Decide today to take an honest look at your finances by learning and applying the simple principles of financial success. The *Financial Fitness Pack* provides you with all the tools needed to get on a path to becoming fiscally fantastic!

Pack includes the Financial Fitness *book, a companion workbook, and 8 audio recordings.*